HOMEWORK

Motivation and Learning Preference

EUNSOOK HONG and ROBERTA M. MILGRAM

Bergin & Garvey
Westport, Connecticut • London

Library of Congress Cataloging-in-Publication Data

Hong, Eunsook.
    Homework : motivation and learning preference / Eunsook Hong and Roberta M.
    Milgram.
       p. cm.
    Includes bibliographical references and index.
    ISBN 0–89789–585–1 (alk. paper)
      1. Homework—Psychological aspects. 2. Motivation in education. I. Milgram,
    Roberta M. II. Title.
    LB1048.H69   2000
    370.15'4—dc21   99–056459

British Library Cataloguing in Publication Data is available.

Library of Congress Catalog Card Number: 99–056459
ISBN: 0–89789–585–1

First published in 2000

Bergin & Garvey, 88 Post Road West, Westport, CT 06881
An imprint of Greenwood Publishing Group, Inc.
www.greenwood.com

Printed in the United States of America

The paper used in this book complies with the
Permanent Paper Standard issued by the National
Information Standards Organization (Z39.48–1984).

10 9 8 7 6 5 4 3 2 1

For Robert Sorgenfrei and Noach (Norman) Milgram,
in gratitude for their insight, support, and patience

Contents

Illustrations

Preface

This book focuses on homework, a topic of popular interest that is not well represented in the professional literature. Both the popular and the research literature have focused on homework as viewed from the outside, that is, on the nature of the homework itself. The focus here is on homework from the inside, on the student who does the homework. The goals of this book are to (a) give counselors, teachers, and parents a theoretical understanding of homework; (b) provide them with a way to assess each student's motivation to do homework and personal profile of home learning preferences; and (c) introduce them to methods and materials designed to facilitate their meeting the formidable challenge of helping children do their homework more effectively. Another important goal of the book is to open up a new research topic that has been almost totally neglected until now. The book consists of 10 chapters and is divided into three parts.

PART I

A conceptual model of homework performance, presented in the first chapter, is the first such model to appear in the literature. It depicts the formulation of the component concepts of the source and strength of motivation to do homework and the profile of preferences about how, when, where, and with whom homework is to be done. The theoretical model is designed to be heuristic, that is, not only to describe the phenomenon of homework, but also to serve as a catalyst for further research on the topic. The second chapter describes the development and the validation of the questionnaire, the Homework Motivation and Preference Questionnaire, that operationally defines the concepts and provides a way to assess them.

PART II

In Part II, the programmatic research that has been conducted on the topic of homework is summarized and integrated. In reading these chapters, it is striking to realize how few previous studies were conducted. Presented and discussed here is an instrument developed in the course of the programmatic research that provides empirical support for the model of homework introduced in the first part of the book. We distinguish between in-school and out-of-school learning styles, and compare learners of different age, gender, achievement level, and culture. We investigate the disparity that exists in many learners between the way they prefer to do their homework and the way they actually do it and consider the role of parent awareness of children's homework style as a possible cause of the disparity. Research was conducted on the relationship of homework motivation and preference to attitudes toward homework and homework achievement in regular children and we also examined the homework preference of gifted and talented students. Many educational benefits accrue from understanding the wide range of individual differences in doing homework and from encouraging children to learn at home under conditions that match their preferences as much as possible.

PART III

The importance of the three-way partnership, student–teacher–parent, and the critical role of teachers and parents in understanding, assessing, and applying students' homework motivation and preference in efforts to improve their attitudes and homework achievement is highlighted in this section. Homework is a double-edged sword: Parent–child conflict rather than cooperation about homework has been the rule, converting what should be a positive and rewarding aspect of parent–child interactions into a battleground on which other problems in the relationship are fought out. Similarly, homework can be a highly useful tool used by teachers to improve academic achievement or a waste of time and effort. It can contribute a great deal, but often contributes little, to the realization of school goals.

Teachers and parents—and possibly students—are keenly aware of the importance of homework in learning, but have been stymied by the paucity of well-grounded information on how to understand and accommodate individual homework styles. This book is designed to provide information to teachers about customizing homework assignments and to parents about designing a homework environment that will match their children's individual homework style. We hope the book will stimulate teachers and parents to work together to create homework assignments and environments in which to do them that will be both enjoyable for parents and children and productive in achieving the goals of education.

ACKNOWLEDGMENTS

We would like to acknowledge a debt to Professor Rita Dunn of St. John's University in New York. Her work on in-school learning styles provided us with the impetus to pursue this further. We thank the University of Nevada, Las Vegas for support of a faculty development leave year for the senior author. We also would like to acknowledge the extensive cooperation of the school personnel and pupils, without whose assistance and participation in our homework studies our book could not have resulted. Special thanks go to Ji-eun Lee and Kit-hung Lee for their many hours of translating the homework scale. Finally, we each wish to express deep gratitude to our husbands, Robert Sorgenfrei and Noach (Norman) Milgram, for their patience, help, and support.

PART I

A MODEL OF HOMEWORK PERFORMANCE AND INSTRUMENT VALIDATION

1

Understanding Homework

Jonathan was dutifully doing his homework assignments while listening to music from the radio at the same time. It is reasonable to expect that his mother would reward his efforts with a smile and encouraging words. It was, therefore, surprising to hear her say, "Really, Jonathan, how can you expect to do your work properly with the radio playing that kind of music?" This incident with minor variations is repeated regularly in many homes all over the world. This incident occurs because parents assume that there are certain conditions that provide the best environment for doing homework, and background music is not among them. Jonathan's mother would be surprised to learn that there are a wide variety of individual differences in the environment in which children prefer to do homework. Some learners do their homework well with music in the background. Music actually helps them concentrate.

The goal of this book is to help Jonathan, his mother, and many other families understand the psychology of the homework process and to cope more successfully with required homework assignments; and to encourage professional educators and researchers to apply and evaluate the applications of a new model of Homework Motivation and Preference. Both the popular and the research literature have focused on homework as viewed from the outside, that is, on the nature of the homework itself. We focus on homework as viewed from the inside, by the student doing the assignments. Many educational benefits will accrue from understanding the wide range of individual differences among learners in the way they prefer to do their homework and from encouraging children to learn at home under conditions that match their preferences as much as possible.

Although much learning occurs in school, a great deal of learning also occurs outside that environment. Homework is a kind of out-of-school learning that has not yet received the serious attention that it merits in the research literature. Learning at school and at home are similar in several ways. The student's ability to learn does not change. The same level of intellectual ability is used to learn at home and at school. Overall motivation to learn is probably highly similar in both settings. The teacher determines what is to be learned both at home and at school. Learning at school and at home are also different in several ways. In-school learning is affected by variables not found in the out-of-school learning situation: The quality of the teacher–learner interaction, the dynamics of the classroom group, and other characteristics of the school in which learning takes place. Similarly, out-of-school learning at home is affected by a myriad of additional and unique factors not found in school: The characteristics of the home environment; the influence of parents, siblings, and friends; and the existence of other activities that compete for the children's time, attention, and effort. However, the major difference between learning at school and at home is that the learner has choices not only about whether to do the homework at all, but also about the circumstances and surroundings in which to do it. As is seen here, there are important individual differences between learners both in motivation to do homework in general, and in specific preferences about when, where, how, and with whom they prefer to do it.

To the best of our knowledge, this book is the first to report on a new direction in research on homework, one that distinguishes between learning at school and at home, and focuses not on the homework itself but on the child doing the homework. This topic has received very little attention in the educational research literature so far. This chapter presents a conceptualization of the complex pattern of motivational, perceptual, and personal–social characteristics, associated with homework behavior and explains the need for an instrument to assess these characteristics. The chapter is divided into four sections:

The first section summarizes previous empirical research on homework, most of which focuses on the homework–academic achievement relationship, and explains the need for a new approach to the topic.

The second section presents the conceptual framework for our approach to the study of homework. It provides the background for understanding the chapters that follow in which we present the research studies we conducted that led to the crystallization of the current conceptualization of homework.

The third section deals with the operational definition and assessment of the motives and the preferences that activate and direct homework behavior. When these motives and preferences are recognized and respected, they increase the probability that an individual will continue to work on and finish homework.

The fourth section presents the implications of the conceptualization and assessment of homework motivation and preferences for students, parents, teachers, and counselors.

UNDERSTANDING HOMEWORK: PAST PERSPECTIVES AND RESEARCH

Homework is assigned, often on a daily basis, to students of all ages all over the world. Planning and assigning homework are a major responsibility and challenge to teachers at all grade levels. Cooper (1989a) defined *homework* as tasks assigned to learners by their teachers, that are to be done outside of school time and without concomitant teacher direction. Homework is most frequently done at home and alone, but it may be done in other places such as the library, in study periods during or after school, or with other people such as parents or fellow students. There are different kinds of homework. Some homework is designed to assure that students review, practice, and drill material that has been learned at school. Other homework assignments are intended to provide students with the opportunity to amplify, elaborate, and enrich previously learned information. Homework is also sometimes used to prepare, in advance, material to be learned in the following classes.

The scope and depth of the literature on the topic of homework may be described in terms that Mark Twain used to describe the Mississippi River. It is "a mile wide and an inch deep." There is a large popular literature consisting of books and articles advising parents and teachers on how to help children with homework (e.g., Bursuck, 1995; Doyle & Barber, 1990; Rosemond, 1990; Wood, 1987), but only a sparse empirical research literature on the topic. Negative articles about homework are ubiquitous in popular periodicals with wide audiences. An article in the January 25, 1999 issue of *Time* magazine entitled "The Homework Ate My Family" and subtitled "Kids are Dazed, Parents are Stressed," is an excellent example of this literature.

Strong opinions on the topic of the efficacy of homework as a teaching strategy appear in the professional literature as well (e.g., Cooper, 1989a; Corno, 1996; Gill & Scholssman, 1996; Palardy, 1995). The views range from strong criticism of the use of homework (Jones & Ross, 1964; Reese, 1995) to claims that the proper use of homework can yield a significant increase in the level of academic achievement (Cooper, 1994; Keith, 1986; Maeroff, 1989, 1992; Paschal, Weinstein, & Walberg, 1984; Walberg, 1984). By contrast, there have been relatively few empirical studies on the effects of homework. A number of authorities on the topic examined these studies and concluded that (a) only a small number of studies have been conducted, (b) many of them were poorly designed, and (c) they focused almost exclusively on the characteristics of the homework itself (e.g., types, quality, amount, grading system, feedback) or on the effect of homework on achievement (Cooper, 1989b; Cooper, Lindsay, Nye, & Greathouse, 1998; Paschal et al., 1984).

Moreover, studies of the effect of homework on academic achievement yield inconsistent findings. For example, a significant, positive effect of homework on student achievement was reported at the high school and college levels (e.g., Cooper et al., 1998; Doyle & Barber, 1990; Keith, 1998; Keith & Benson, 1992; Keith, Reimers, Fehrmann, Pottebaum, & Aubey, 1986). However, at the elementary school level, findings are inconsistent: Some studies report a positive effect of homework on academic achievement (e.g., Paschal et al., 1984), whereas others find no difference in student achievement as a function of time spent on homework (Chen & Stevenson, 1989; Cool & Keith, 1991; Smith, 1990). Some investigators even found a negative relationship between amount of homework and student attitudes toward homework (Cooper et al., 1998).

A recent study (Cooper et al., 1998) found that it was not the amount of homework assigned but rather the amount of homework completed that is associated with student achievement, especially at the upper grades. They also reported that about one third of the students do not finish their homework. These findings serve as a warning sign that an important influence on the homework–achievement relationship has been ignored and merits systematic investigations.

If degree of compliance is a major determinant of the efficacy of homework in enhancing achievement, questions of what increases the degree of compliance merit high priority in future research. Considerable evidence indicates that allowing children to learn in school under conditions that match their individual preferences yield higher achievement and improved attitudes toward school (e.g., Dunn, Beaudry, & Klavas, 1989; Dunn & Milgram, 1993). Unfortunately, there have been no studies about whether matching individual out-of-school learning preferences with the conditions under which homework is done increases compliance with these assignments, raises homework achievement, or both. One of the major reasons why this question has not been investigated is the lack of a theoretical framework that provides a heuristic conceptual model to stimulate research on homework, in general, and the lack of a reliable instrument to assess individual homework behavior, in particular.

Research studies on the intrapersonal and interpersonal characteristics of the person doing the homework (e.g., source and level of motivation, individual preferences of time, place, conditions, etc.) have been conducted even less frequently than research on homework assignment characteristics and their effects on academic achievement. School administrators, teachers, parents, and researchers in the field are acutely aware of individual personality characteristics of children in the school learning process. They recognize that it is not enough to be able to learn, that is, to have the intellectual ability to master the material, but that a person must want to learn and be able to persevere until an academic assignment is completed or an academic goal is achieved. This understanding has led to continuing efforts to understand motivation, in general, and to investigate the personal–social characteristics that affect learning in school, in particular. The time has come to expand this understanding to out-of-school learning. This book is a first step in that direction.

Cognitive Style, Learning Style, and Home Learning Style

It is important to distinguish between *cognitive style, school learning style*, and *home learning style*. Unfortunately, these concepts have been confounded both theoretically and empirically. With the development of cognitive psychology and its emphasis on the cognitive processes of perceiving, remembering, and problem solving, a number of investigators conceptualized different aspects of individual cognitive style in information processing and learning. Examples of this approach may be found in the Study Process Questionnaire (Biggs, 1979), Learning Style Inventory (Kolb, 1976), Inventory of Learning Process (Schmeck, Ribich, & Ramanaih, 1977) and in Field Dependence–Independence measures (Witkin & Goodenough, 1977). Investigators of cognitive style did not clearly distinguish between cognitive style and learning style. Moreover, they did not investigate cognitive style as a function of the setting in which learning takes place, in or out of school. It is reasonable to assume that cognitive style characteristics would not differ as a function of setting, but this assumption remains to be empirically demonstrated. In-depth investigations of individual differences in cognitive processing are indeed warranted, but these topics fall beyond the limits of the subject matter in this volume.

There is a major difference in research on learning style as compared to cognitive style. Research on cognitive style has not focused on the effect of individual interpersonal and intrapersonal characteristics on learning. By contrast, research on learning style has focused on the profile of children's personal–social and situational preferences for learning in the formal school setting. Dunn and Dunn (1972) presented a theoretical model of learning style and Dunn, Dunn, and Price (1984) developed the Learning Style Inventory (LSI) that operationally defines and assesses 23 of the conceptualized components of learning style. According to this approach, each person's learning style consists of a unique combination of strengths and weaknesses on elements that reflect various aspects of the environmental, emotional, sociological, and physical conditions under which a person acquires new knowledge and skills. The Dunn and Dunn learning style model and the LSI are described in detail elsewhere (Dunn & Dunn, 1992, 1993; Dunn, Dunn, & Price, 1987), but a few examples of the approach are in order. The environmental elements include high versus low preference for sound or light while learning; the emotional elements, extent of motivation and persistence; the sociological elements, the preference to learn alone or with others; the physical elements, the time of day when one likes to learn and one's preferred perceptual channel, such as auditory or visual. Dunn and Dunn (1992, 1993) summarized the findings of a large number of research studies that demonstrated that when children were allowed to learn in school under conditions that matched their learning style preferences, their academic achievement and their attitudes toward school improved.

Dunn and Dunn's (1972) theoretical model of learning style also includes such psychological elements of learning style as global versus analytic and impulsive versus reflective styles of thinking, and right versus left hemispheric dominance. In their model they do not distinguish between cognitive style, learning style, and the personality characteristics presumed to be associated with these two variables. The cognitive style elements cited in their learning style formulation are not measured by the instrument that they developed to assess learning style.

In several studies, college students were taught how to use information on their learning style when doing their homework (Clark-Thayer, 1987; Dunn, Deckinger, Withers, & Katzenstein, 1990; Lenehan, Dunn, Inghan, Signer, & Murray, 1994). Improved academic performance was reported for students who did their homework under conditions that matched their learning style, that is, for example, at their best time of day, and in an environment responsive to their individual preferences for sound, light, formal or informal design of furniture. In these studies, the students were administered the LSI and given feedback on their preferred learning style.

Neither cognitive nor learning style theorists distinguish between learning at school and learning at home. This means that they assume an individual's motivation and personal preferences for learning in school and for learning out of school are the same. It is remarkable that no one has seriously questioned this assumption. A major difference between home and school learning is the physical presence of the teacher at school, but not at home. The teacher has influence on learning even when it takes place at home in that he or she determines the amount of homework assigned and the specific demands of each assignment. On the other hand, learning at home is done outside of school hours (i.e., a different time of day or on weekends), and is influenced by parents, siblings, and other children. Hong, Milgram, and Perkins (1995) and Perkins and Milgram (1996) distinguished theoretically and empirically between in-school learning style and out-of-school learning or homework style. They used different questionnaires of learning preferences in the two settings and found that learning style and homework style are correlated, but not empirically equivalent, and that different patterns of homework style are found in high versus low homework achievers and in children with positive versus negative attitudes toward homework.

In summary, individual students have both a characteristic school learning style, and a somewhat related, but not equivalent, characteristic style for doing their homework outside of school. These two kinds of preferences should be assessed separately because of their implications for optimal academic performance. As indicated earlier, when children are allowed to learn in school under conditions that match their learning style preferences, they have higher academic achievement and more positive attitudes toward school (Dunn, 1989; Dunn & Milgram, 1993). Therefore, it is reasonable to expect that if children do their homework under conditions that match their preferences, similar positive results will be obtained. The goal of this book is to provide teachers, parents, and children with a basic understanding of the homework process, in general, and individual *home learning style*, in particular. Such understanding has an important practical implication in that it can provide the basis for developing individualized practical strategies that can help learners meet homework requirements more successfully and more enjoyably.

UNDERSTANDING HOMEWORK: NEW PERSPECTIVES AND RESEARCH

What Is Homework Performance?

Homework performance may be defined as the process that occurs when a learner begins, makes continued effort to work on, and completes at home or in another out-of-school setting, the learning tasks assigned at school. Each learner has a distinct, personal homework performance pattern that consists of a unique profile of motivation and preferences that influence compliance with and completion of the requirements of homework tasks. This definition clearly reflects our emphasis on the characteristics of the student doing the homework and not those of the homework itself. Homework assignments may be performed well or poorly. The concept of homework performance does not refer to good performance only, but rather to the full range of performance from well done to poorly done.

Homework by definition takes place without concomitant teacher direction. In school, the learner is part of a class group and learns in a certain way usually determined by the teacher, occasionally by a group of students and only rarely by the individual student. By contrast, when it comes to homework, learners have choices. First of all, they can decide whether to do the homework at all and how much time and effort to invest in doing the assigned tasks. Once they have made these decisions, they can choose to do homework in a variety of ways and presumably do it the way they like. There are a wide variety of individual differences in homework performance among learners both in the source and strength of motivation to do homework, and in preferences about what, when, where, how, and with whom they like to do it. We developed a conceptual model designed to comprehend, explain, and improve the homework process for the benefit of learners, teachers, and parents.

A Conceptual Model of Homework Performance: Why?

Until now, our research on homework has used a bottom–up or inductive approach. Our studies that focus on the personal–social characteristics of the child doing the homework are described in detail in the chapters that follow. We first established that in-school learning style and out-of-school homework style are empirically distinguishable (Hong et al., 1995; Perkins & Milgram, 1996). We examined homework preferences in children of three age groups and in four different cultures (Hong, 1998; Hong & Lee, 1999a, 1999b; Hong et al., 1995; Hong et al., 2000; Hong, Tomoff, Wozniak, Carter, & Topham, 2000; Ohayon, 1999). We investigated whether children's preferred home learning styles differ from their actual homework learning styles (Hong & Milgram, 1999). We also examined the homework preferences of children who were intellectually gifted or highly creative in their thinking (Ohayon, 1999). In each study, we investigated the validity and reliability of the measure used to assess individual homework motivation and preferences and improved its psychometric characteristics. As you read these chapters, please bear in mind that later studies reflect changes in the instruments used over the course of this programmatic research.

In these initial studies, we followed the lead of Dunn and Dunn (1972) and used the terminology of learning style. In the course of our work, it became clear that the learning style model confounds a number of important concepts. First, as explained earlier, the concepts of cognitive and learning style were confounded. Second, in-school and out-of-school learning were confounded. Finally, the source and strength of the motivational components that determine if one will perform homework assignments were inaccurately depicted as preferences and confounded with the environmental, intrapersonal, and interpersonal preferences that affect why one continues to make the effort required to successfully finish homework tasks.

We developed a new conceptual model entitled Homework Performance: Motivation and Preference, based on research findings that started with the tentative conceptual framework mentioned earlier. We do not view this conceptual model of homework performance as a finished product, but rather one that will be modified according to experience with it in the field. The conceptual model of homework performance presented in detail later clearly distinguishes between cognitive style and learning style, in-school and out-of-school learning, and motivation to do homework, on the one hand, and preferences among a wide variety of conditions that affect the success and satisfaction with which homework is done, on the other.

HOMEWORK PERFORMANCE: MOTIVATION AND PREFERENCE

Homework Performance: Motivation and Preference

Our conceptual model of Homework Performance is presented in Figure 1.1. The conceptual components of homework performance may be divided into two categories, motivation and preference. The first category, *motivation*, postulates the source and strength of the motives that explain the initial activation of the process of doing the required homework assignments. This category offers possible answers to the most basic questions: Why do learners comply at all with the teacher's request that they do their homework and with the instructions about how to do them? What influences whether or not a learner will start and willingly perform homework? The second category, *preference*, influences the degree to which the learner will proceed and continue homework efforts until finished. What are the intrapersonal and interpersonal preferences of the individual about how, where, when, and with whom to do homework? The match of the demand characteristics of the homework assignments themselves, as determined by the teacher, with the level of motivation and the pattern of interpersonal and intrapersonal preferences of the learner doing the homework determines whether the goals of homework will be accomplished.

Homework Performance Motivation

The category of motivation in the Homework Performance model may be further divided into two subcategories, *sources* and *strength*. Three sources of motivation to perform homework are formulated. A learner may be *self-motivated*, *parent-motivated*, and/or *teacher-motivated*. These three components are not mutually exclusive. A learner's motivation to perform homework may be influenced by one, two, or three sources in degrees.

Figure 1.1
Homework Performance: Motivation and Preference

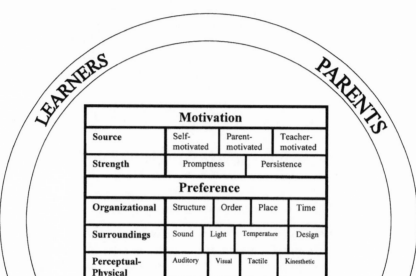

(1) Self-motivated refers to an individual's personal and intrinsic willingness to learn at home.

(2) Parent-motivated refers to the efforts of learners to do their homework in order to satisfy their parents. The degree to which parents motivate their children to do homework is frequently a consequence of parental intervention and involvement. Parents who demonstrate interest in homework, offer reasonable help as required, and provide appropriate rewards and reinforcement for consistent and successful homework performance, can increase motivation to do homework. Conversely, parents who give no attention to homework performance and give the impression that they do not consider it important can lower homework motivation. Finally, parents who are over-involved with their children's homework may produce a conflict situation that negatively

affects the parent–child relationship as well as the child's homework motivation.

(3) Teacher-motivated refers to students devoting time and effort to the homework tasks in order to satisfy their teachers. High motivation to perform homework may reflect the overall teacher–pupil relationship. If the relationship is highly positive in a variety of ways, doing the homework that that teacher assigns is one way to express regard and respect for the teacher and to earn the respect of the teacher. Conversely, teachers may be responsible for low motivation to perform homework.

Strength, the second subcategory of Homework Performance Motivation, has two components, *promptness* and *persistence*. These relatively stable personality characteristics reflect the strength of the learner's motivation to perform homework. They influence when the effort is initiated and to what degree it is maintained.

(1) Promptness refers to the tendency of a learner to do homework immediately when assigned and procrastination to the inclination to delay starting the process. The time that elapses between receiving assignments and starting to do them is viewed as an indicator of strength of motivation. Strong homework performance motivation is evidenced by immediate attention to the assignments. Weak motivation is reflected in procrastination, that is, in delays that vary from starting the assignment late in the time available to complete it to doing it at the last minute or not at all. Research on promptness versus procrastination has focused on the causes of the phenomenon and to a lesser extent on its relationship to school achievement, with little attention to homework achievement (Ferrari, Johnson, & McCown, 1995).

(2) Persistence refers to the degree of sustained effort maintained in the process of doing homework. Learners differ as to the amount of continuous time that they spend on homework. Some begin and proceed with the homework, without interruption, until they finish. Others cannot tolerate concentrated effort and are inclined to do their homework in a large number of short time periods. Such sporadic starts and stops are likely to be less efficient.

Homework Performance Preference

The preference category may be divided into four subcategories: *organizational, surroundings, perceptual-physical,* and *interpersonal.*

Organizational

There are four organizational components, *structure, order, place,* and *time.* These components represent individual preferences about what homework is to be done, in what order, where, and when, respectively. They are defined here.

(1) Structure. Structure of the homework refers to the learner's preference for the kinds of instructions that the teacher gives about how the homework is to be done. Homework may be highly structured, well defined, highly specific, and may only have one way to do it correctly. By contrast, homework tasks may be relatively unstructured, open-ended, with many ways to complete the assignment correctly. Learners may prefer more or less structured homework tasks, but teachers determine the degree of structure of homework assignments. If learners were provided with structure options in doing homework assignments, some more and some less structured, the motivation to do homework and the quality of homework performance would probably increase.

(2) Order. The learner has much more choice when it comes to the organization of how, where, and when the homework is done. Learners have preferences in each of these and, depending on circumstances and parental pressures and sensibilities, usually can exercise them. There are individual differences between learners as to the order in which they prefer to do their homework assignments in the different subjects. Some children prefer to do the tasks that are easiest for them first and get them out of the way. Others prefer to tackle the difficult assignments to begin with, while their energy level is highest. Preference about order is also influenced by how much the learner likes one subject over another. Some learners prefer to do homework assignments in the subjects they like first and leave the least liked for last. Others prefer to leave the attractive subjects for last as a reward for having completed the less attractive subjects. The order component does not refer to the kind of order that each learner prefers (e.g., the easy assignments first and the difficult ones last), but rather to whether he or she maintains a stable, unchanged order pattern on a regular basis or whether he or she varies the pattern (e.g., sometimes easy–difficult and at other times, difficult–easy).

(3) Place. Homework can be done in a variety of places at home. A child's own room, the living room, the kitchen are all frequent settings for doing homework. It can also be done in school: in the library or in the classroom in special supervised study periods. Here again, we are interested in variability versus regularity. Is it always the same place in the house or outside the house, or does the preferred place vary? Does the learner stay in one place to do the homework or does he or she find it difficult to utilize one place and prefer various places?

(4) Time. The organizational component of time represents whether homework is done at a fixed time each day or whether the time for homework is not constant but rather can change from day to day.

Surroundings

Doing homework requires continued effort. The surroundings under which the homework is done influences the degree to which the learner sustains the effort required to successfully complete the homework tasks. In school, the learner has little choice about the surroundings in which learning takes place. At home, the learner has more choice about the general surroundings in which to do homework and can often adjust *sound, light, temperature,* and/or *design* to his or her liking. Preferences for homework surroundings also vary greatly among individuals. Some prefer a setting that is as quiet as possible, whereas others find background sound relaxing and helpful. Very bright versus dim lighting and warm versus cool temperature are additional surrounding characteristics that make a lot of difference to some learners when doing their homework. The design of the room in which homework is being done can also make a difference. Some learners like formal furniture, a desk and straight chair, whereas others prefer an easy chair or even a thick rug on which they can relax and work. For practical reasons, it is unlikely that individual preferences of sound, light, temperature, and design will be matched by the circumstances of any school classroom, and much more so in the crowded classrooms in most schools today. It is much more possible for parents to adjust the surroundings in which their children do homework, if they are aware of their children's preferences and able and willing to match them.

Perceptual-Physical

There are six components under this category: *Auditory, visual, tactile, kinesthetic, intake,* and *mobility.* It is a difficult but worthwhile challenge for creative teachers to individualize homework in terms of the perceptual-physical preferences of the learners. It is less difficult but equally valuable for parents to make arrangements for doing homework that meet the student's physical needs. There are a wide variety of ways that these preferences can be taken into account. A few examples of what can be done are proposed here.

(1) Auditory. Some children prefer homework assignments that require them to listen to tapes or CDs that contain material to be used in doing the homework, and also prefer to hear homework instructions.

(2) Visual. Other learners prefer assignments that involve reading or watching films, and prefer to see written homework instructions.

(3) Tactile. Some children prefer the "hands-on" type of homework. They enjoy preparing exhibits to display for their classmates, building things and similar homework activities that require them to actually touch and manipulate materials.

(4) Kinesthetic. Some learners like homework that involves firsthand experience and active participation in events or activities that lead to the accumulation of knowledge: observing a phenomenon, interviewing an interesting person, or conducting an experiment. A learner, for example, could be assigned to use a computer to go on a virtual trip to a certain

country studied in school, and the homework could be to report on a specific aspect of life there.

(5) Intake. This component reflects the physical preference to eat, drink, or chew while learning. Intake is very difficult to respect in the school classroom, but relatively simple to permit at home. Learners may prefer to eat or drink while they learn for a number of reasons. The simple explanation is that they like to get nourishment when they are doing other things rather than in the more formal setting in which we usually think of people eating, that is, sitting at a table and eating a meal. For example, it has become routine in many homes for family members to eat individually in front of the TV rather than together. It is, therefore, understandable how some learners might prefer to eat or drink while doing their homework. Some learners filter unwanted thoughts while doing homework by chewing or eating, but not for the purpose of satisfying their biological need for nourishment. Like the background music that help some learners concentrate on their tasks, the chewing activity can have the similar effect.

(6) Mobility. Some children prefer to sit in the same place while doing their homework, whereas others prefer to take time out occasionally or frequently to move to different places in the house before resuming doing their homework. The mobility component is another perceptual-physical preference that can more easily be accommodated at home and with only the greatest difficulty at school.

Interpersonal Preferences

Some learners prefer to do their homework alone, whereas others prefer to do it in the company of others. Within the second category, there are two kinds of interpersonal preferences: doing homework alone or with age peers and doing it in the presence of adult authority figures or without such a person around. A learner may like to work alone, with one other age peer (i.e., in a pair), or with a group (i.e., with more than one same-age peer). Similarly, a learner may prefer to do homework in the presence of authority figures such as parents, parentlike figures, or older siblings. These people may offer help and advice with the homework or they may serve as a source of support and encouragement while the learner does the homework.

Assessing Homework Performance

We operationally defined the component concepts and developed the Homework Motivation and Preference Questionnaire (HMPQ; Hong & Milgram, 1998), to assess these variables and validate them empirically. The instrument yields an individual Homework Motivation and Preference Profile (HMPP) that provides a visual and verbal representation of the profile. The components and the interpretation of low versus high scores are listed in Table 1.1. Middle level scores indicate no strong preference in either direction.

CONCLUSIONS

Homework is a powerful tool that can contribute to the advancement of children's education and knowledge or it can do more damage than good to these enterprises. The difference between the two outcomes depends on the quality of the decisions as to how homework is implemented. Homework, if properly used, may be the most effective and cost-efficient way to solve some of the most difficult educational problems. Proper use of homework can lead to significant improvement in academic achievement. Homework is an ongoing enterprise in all academic settings, it is there to be used and does not have to be discovered or invented. However, in its current form it is often part of the problem and not part of the solution. In order for homework to become a positive and powerful force in education, change will have to take place about how homework is understood, how it is used in schools, and how it is done at home.

In this opening chapter, we have focused on understanding homework and suggested a conceptual model to explain the phenomenon. We developed the theory of homework performance in order to provide a rationale, general principles, general concepts and their respective components and to improve homework as an educational tool. In order to succeed in improving homework, the close cooperation of three distinct groups is required: the teachers who give the homework and afterwards grade it; the students who do the homework, derive benefits from doing it and from the feedback about their homework performance from their teachers; and the parents who largely control the physical and psychological surroundings in which their children do their homework and enjoy a more serene and conflict-free home environment if their children do their homework in an efficient and personally gratifying manner.

The role of teachers in homework is not to be underestimated. Teachers have a major role to play in improving homework because teacher instructions determine its content, scope, and specific requirements. It has been clearly established that higher academic achievement and improved attitudes result from tailoring the learning experiences to the cognitive and personal–social characteristics of the learner. Individualizing learning at school and at home is a difficult but not impossible challenge. In suggesting intervention strategies in the coming chapters, we discuss how teachers' practice in the classroom affects homework.

Table 1.1

Homework Motivation and Preference Profile (HMPP): Interpretation of Low versus High Scores

Components	Low Scores	High Scores
Motivation source		
1. Self-motivated	weak	Strong
2. Parent-motivated	weak	Strong
3. Teacher-motivated	weak	Strong
Motivation strength		
4. Promptness	procrastinates	prompt
5. Persistence	low	high
Organizational		
6. Structure	prefers unstructured	prefers structure
7. Order	variable order	set order
8. Place	variable place	set place
9. Time	variable time	set time
Surroundings		
10. Sound	prefers quiet	prefers sound
11. Light	prefers dim	prefers bright
12. Temperature	prefers cool	prefers warm
13. Design	prefers informal	prefers formal
Perceptual-physical		
14. Auditory	does not prefer	prefers
15. Visual	does not prefer	prefers
16. Tactile	does not prefer	prefers
17. Kinesthetic	does not prefer	prefers
18. Intake	does not prefer	prefers
19. Mobility	does not prefer	prefers
Interpersonal		
20. Alone-Peers	prefers to work alone	prefers to work with peers
21. Authority figures	does not want present	wants present

For example, if learners have not done group homework assignments in school, it will be difficult for them to do homework cooperatively in groups outside of the classrooms. Similarly, if teachers do not use hands-on and experiential type learning activities in school so that learners become familiar with them, it will be difficult for students to do assignments that use these approaches at home.

School and home learning are to be viewed as closely related, and ideally should be carried out with teachers, learners, and parents working cooperatively and collaboratively. Efforts to match preferred and actual modes of learning should take place both in school and at home. Preservice and in-service teacher training should include training in ways to individualize assignments both for work at school and at home in order to create options that recognize individual differences among learners. Parents have an equally important role to play in improving the homework situation. They have a small number of children to deal with and not a large class. They are very interested in the academic achievement of their own children, much more than even the most devoted teacher can be interested in any particular child.

In summary, teachers, parents, and students are equally important in determining the degree to which homework is effective in meeting its goals. In order for homework to function properly, they must work together as a team. Teachers assign homework, parents provide the environment in which it is done, and finally, students, each with a unique profile of motivation and preference for learning, do the homework. This three-way partnership and its effect on homework performance was depicted in Figure 1.1. It is a challenge to parents, teachers, principals, and counselors to cooperate and to share information about children's homework motivation and preference profile and to develop strategies to be used at school and at home to attain a better match between what the child likes to do and has to do when learning. The chapters that follow assist teachers and parents in meeting this challenge for their own satisfaction and for the ultimate benefit of the students. We discuss many aspects of homework, present an integrative summary of the results of our investigations of homework performance, and suggest practical strategies for parents and teachers to use this knowledge to make homework performance of children more effective and more enjoyable.

2

Profiling Homework Motivation and Preference

The conceptual model of homework performance presented in chapter 1 consists of two major categories (motivation and preference), with six subcategories and 21 components. We developed an instrument designed to assess the components of homework performance and subjected it to an extensive validation process. Although teachers and parents may be able to observe certain patterns of learning preference and motivation levels of children, some component learning preferences are not readily observable and the behaviors associated with them are often misinterpreted. For example, a child who cannot sit quietly in his or her chair at a desk is often viewed as troublesome and not wanting to do the homework. However, it might be that this child needs to move about in the room or from room to room or prefers to do homework in an informal arrangement such as sitting on a sofa or in a lounge chair or sprawled on a rug on the floor.

It is a challenge to correctly identify the optimal conditions that will help students do their homework successfully and enjoyably, on one hand, and to recognize the reasons for student homework difficulties, on the other. In order to meet the challenge, it is important to have correct information about homework motivation and preference. To obtain correct information, a reliable and valid assessment instrument is needed. Because the information we seek is the pattern of self-perceived preferences, a self-report measure can be used in the assessment process. Whether the preferences for doing homework are the same as those actually used is an interesting and important question that is discussed in depth in the next chapter.

As with all self-report instruments, the validity of the assessment of homework motivation and preference is based on the assumption that learners are aware of, perceive, and can report their own preferences accurately. Because one can never be sure that the data gathered is completely accurate, it is especially important to provide evidence that the instrument used to collect data demonstrates a reasonable degree of reliability and validity. As with other instruments, some students may be tired during the administration, not focused on the task at hand, or reluctant to share their views on homework. Accordingly, they may not respond to the questionnaire in complete sincerity. Additionally, a student may misinterpret one or more of the items and thus distort the assessment. The Homework Motivation and Preference Questionnaire (HMPQ) is designed to yield a profile of each student's homework motivation and preference and to serve as a guide for adjusting homework assignments for individual learners. Accordingly, users should exercise particular caution to establish the reliability of responses not only for the entire group but for individual students as well.

This chapter presents the background and history of the development and validation of the HMPQ and describes the modification and revision process that has taken place. The instrument is ready to be used for student assessment; however, the process of modification and validation will progress.

DEVELOPMENT AND VALIDATION OF THE HOMEWORK MOTIVATION AND PREFERENCE QUESTIONNAIRE (HMPQ)

Many different formulations of the concept of learning styles have been presented and a wide variety of instruments proposed to measure it. The instruments vary in length, format, and number of dimensions of learning style assessed. Some of the tests require special training to administer and interpret, whereas others are relatively simple to use. Among the measures of learning styles that have been widely used are Canfield's Learning Styles Inventory (Canfield & Lafferty, 1976), Dunn, Dunn, and Price's LSI (Dunn et al., 1987), Grasha and Riechmann's Student Learning Styles Questionnaire (Grasha & Riechmann, 1975), Gregorc's Style Delineator (Gregorc, 1982), Hill's Cognitive Style Interest Inventory (Hill, 1976), Keefe and Monk's Learning Style Profile (Keefe & Monk, 1986), and Kolb's Learning Style Inventory (Kolb, 1976).

The authors did not distinguish between learning style and cognitive style in the names of the tests. This reflected the fact that investigators often used the constructs of learning style and cognitive style interchangeably or include one in the other in their theories (e.g., Keefe, 1988). *Learning style* is broadly defined as a learner's perceptions of his or her own preferences for different types of learning conditions, including instructional materials and activities and learning environments. These styles are usually measured by self-report instruments that ask individuals how they prefer to learn. Cognitive styles, on the other hand, focus specifically on the way learners perceive, acquire, and process information that is more closely related to mental work. Cognitive style is assessed by means of task-specific measures of actual mental skills or tendencies in performing those skills (Jonassen & Grabowski, 1993).

Neither learning style nor cognitive style instruments were designed to measure home learning. Accordingly, we developed an instrument to serve that purpose. In defining home learning preferences (see chapter 1), we adopted the broad definition of learning style just cited. The current instrument does not attempt to measure underlying information-processing mechanisms or how these mechanisms are related to home learning preferences. The instrument that we developed can be used in determining the differences in learning preferences in various groups (e.g., high vs. low achievers) but it does not provide information on the reasons (e.g., learners' specific skills) that enable students in these groups to use certain preferred modes of learning.

Numerous investigators addressed the issue of whether self-report learning style inventories are of sufficient psychometric quality to justify their continued use for research or educational practices (e.g., Curry, 1987, 1990; Ferrari et al., 1996; R. Sims, Veres, & Locklear, 1991). It was reported, for example, that a number of widely used learning style tests are not good predictors of academic performance (e.g., Leiden, Crosby, & Follmer, 1990). However, other studies that employed information from learning style inventories found that matching learning activities and environments to individual learning style preferences resulted in increased student achievement (e.g., Callan, 1996; Dunn, Griggs, Olson, Beasley, & Gorman, 1995; Hayes & Allison, 1993; Hodgin & Wooliscroft, 1997; Renzulli & Reis, 1998). A large number of these studies used the Dunn et al. (1987) LSI. These conflicting findings are not unexpected because of the wide variety of other factors that affect educational achievement (e.g., learner traits such as ability, prior knowledge; external factors such as socioeconomic status of the family, peer influence). The effect or predictive value of learning style information is probably quite modest, even when learning preferences have significant impacts on student learning.

Although there is a large literature on both learning styles and homework, there have been few studies of the relationship between the two. The small number of studies that were conducted on the effects of matching homework environment to students' learning preferences used an in-school learning style questionnaire to measure out-of-school learning preferences (Clark-Thayer, 1987; Dunn, et al., 1990). One reason for using in-school learning style measures in studies of home learning research was the lack of an instrument designed specifically to assess individual profiles of home learning preference. In light of the finding that learning styles in school and out of school were related yet empirically distinguishable (Hong, Milgram, & Perkins, 1995; Perkins & Milgram, 1996), we set out to develop a homework style measure.

We compared the major learning style models and inventories available and found that the LSI (Dunn et al., 1987) was widely used for assessment in elementary and secondary schools and that evidence of high reliability and predictive validity ratings had been reported (Curry, 1987; DeBello, 1990; Dunn & Griggs, 1988; Keefe, 1982). Thus, we initially adopted the Dunn and Dunn (1972) conceptual framework on which the LSI was based. This decision was also based on a number of practical considerations. First, we were interested in developing a comprehensive instrument that would measure a wide variety of aspects relating to home learning situations. Second, the practical consideration of usability was important to us, that is, the ease with which parents and teachers can use the instrument with minimal training.

In summary, the focus was to develop a reliable and valid instrument to investigate the various internal and external learning conditions learners prefer while doing their homework that can be used by teachers at school and parents at home with relative ease.

Dunn and her associates assessed four out of the five categories of preference presented in their learning style model. The names of the categories and the components of each were as follows: (a) environmental: sound, light, temperature, design; (b) emotional: motivation, persistence, responsibility, structure; (c) sociological: alone or with peers, adult figures, varied ways; and (d) physiological: perceptual, intake, time of the day, mobility (Dunn & Dunn, 1992, 1993; Dunn et al., 1987). We did not expect the overall dimensions and specific components of learning style preferences in home situations to correspond exactly to the parallel dimensions and components used for the in-school setting. Nevertheless, we initially developed a homework preference questionnaire largely based on the elements in the Dunn and Dunn (1972) model with a few modifications (see Study 1) and subjected the initial scale to a series of validation studies (see Studies 2–9). The findings of these nine studies provided empirical support for our formulation of homework performance model and led to the development of an improved measure of it.

During the process of providing validity evidence and refining the instrument, we adopted a new name for the questionnaire that was better suited to our model. We decided to call it the Homework Motivation and Preferences Questionnaire; the reasons for the modifications are explained in detail in this chapter. We explored the factor structure of the scale and refined it by examining reliability, item dispersion, and item discrimination indices. Specifically, nine separate studies were conducted over a 5-year period to (a) develop a questionnaire that would have content validity for home learning preference, (b) examine the internal consistency and factor structure of the questionnaire, (c) examine the temporal stability, (d) examine convergent and discriminant validity, and (e) refine the questionnaire based on these studies.

STUDY 1

Overview

We used the definition of homework performance cited in chapter 1 to develop a questionnaire that assesses learners' homework motivation and preference, to define categories, subcategories, and components of the questionnaire, and to generate and refine test items. As indicated earlier, the items were initially derived from the LSI (Dunn et al., 1987), an instrument that is used to assess in-school learning styles. Accordingly, it was necessary to conduct a multistep process of adding, deleting, and modifying items in order to establish an initial item pool that was representative of and relevant to our domain of interest, that is, home learning preferences.

Method

Four steps were employed to identify the components and categories of home learning preferences and to construct items for a homework preference questionnaire.

1. The purposes of the questionnaire development were thoroughly considered to determine whether an adoption and modification of existing instruments would be feasible.
2. The literatures on learning styles and homework were reviewed and analyzed.
3. Previously published learning style scales were examined.
4. A decision was made on whether to develop an entirely new questionnaire or to adopt and modify existing ones.

It was decided that the models that support the goal of the current questionnaire development were the learning style models suggested by Dunn et al., (1987) and Keefe and Monk (1986). These multidimensional models share certain conceptual similarities with those that we aim to assess, and have been widely accepted and used in elementary and secondary schools. Thus, it was decided that we adopt and modify these models and inventories, especially that of Dunn et al. (1987) for the development of a homework preference questionnaire.

Next, some of the items were selected from the existing inventories and some new items were constructed. The initial pool of items was then reviewed. We eliminated and modified redundant and overly simple or confusing items, ensured proper grammatical structure and readability level for school-aged children, varied directionality by providing positive and negative statements where applicable, and ensured that each category had adequate coverage and that each item reflected only one homework preference component. In the process of item development, we considered the length of the questionnaire, thus, trying to limit each component to as small number of items as possible without compromising the psychometric quality of the inventory.

Results

We identified five categories that were thought to encompass principal aspects of homework preferences. The initial categories were environmental, organizational, motivational, perceptual-physical, and sociological. These initial categories represented a substantial departure from those of the learning style model suggested by Dunn and Dunn (1972). The initial item pool consisted of 88 items, with five categories and 21 components:

1. The environmental category consisted of five preference components: sound, light, temperature, design, and place. Each component consisted of 4 items (20 items for this category).

2. The organizational category consisted of two components: structure and set order, with 4 items per component (8 items).

3. The motivational category consisted of 5 components: self-, parent-, and teacher-motivation, persistence, responsibility, with 4 items per component (20 items).

4. The perceptual-physical category consisted of seven components: auditory, visual, tactile, kinesthetic, intake, mobility, time. Each component consisted of 4 items, except for the time component with eight items, with two items each for set time, morning, afternoon, and evening (32 items).

5. The sociological category consisted of 2 components: alone–peers and authority figures. Each component consisted of 4 items (8 items).

Four items that describe preferences in the choice of "place" to study (i.e., using the same place or variable places for homework) were newly generated for the current questionnaire, whereas other items were adopted and modified from the LSI. The questionnaire was titled as the Homework Preference Questionnaire (HPQ) at this stage, and a 5-point Likert format was adopted (i.e., *absolutely disagree, disagree, difficult to decide, agree, absolutely agree*). The HPQ with the proposed or hypothesized five categories were subjected to the validation procedures reported in the studies that follow.

STUDY 2

Overview

The purpose of Study 2 was to examine whether the proposed five-category factor structure of the HPQ can be grounded in the data, using a sample of seventh graders from the United States. The study also examined the internal consistency, item dispersion, and item-total correlations of the HPQ. The scale was refined according to the examination of the findings from these analyses.

Although we suggested the five overarching categories of the 21 components (24 components if the four time-related components—set time, morning, afternoon, evening—are counted separately), some of the components in a category were not expected to converge as a factor. That is, the components within most of the hypothesized categories described in Study 1 are conceptually related, but empirical correlations among components should not be expected to be meaningful in some of the categories. For example, the environmental category consists of five components—sound, light, temperature, design, place—each with distinct characteristics; thus correlations among most of these five components would not be meaningful. On the other hand, the components of the motivational category have meaningful relationships among them. In this case, the components would correlate through their relationship to one or two higher order motivation factors. The factor analyses determined these relationships.

Method

The participants were 263 U.S. seventh graders (127 males and 133 females; 3 unspecified). The students were from a public middle school in a large western metropolitan area. The sample selection was based on voluntary participation, and parent consent forms were obtained from all participating students. The HPQ was group administered to students in their classrooms. The data analyses were conducted on the responses of 263 students for whom there were complete data on the HPQ.

Results

Exploratory Factor Analysis (EFA)

A maximum likelihood factor analysis with varimax rotation was conducted. The number of factors retained was determined by the eigenvalues greater than 1, a minimum of two items for each factor that have loadings greater than .30, and theoretical soundness. Although there were 17 factors with the size of eigenvalues greater than 1, one factor did not have discernible factor loading that is greater than .30, another factor was uninterpretable. A 16-factor solution was also obtained but the last factor was not interpretable. Thus, the 15-factor varimax solution, which accounted for 50% of the variance, was selected.

The number of empirically determined factors (15) was smaller than the number hypothesized (21), indicating that some of the components were correlated highly enough to converge as higher order factors. The items with the loadings greater than .30 were interpreted. Due to the large number of items tested, a summary of the findings is presented here: The first number is the factor number, followed by the empirical factor name, and the quantity and names of original items that loaded on the respective factor. The eigenvalues after the varimax rotation ranged from 1.29 to 5.71.

1. Motivational 1: 11 items including 3 self-motivated, 4 parent-motivated, 3 teacher-motivated, and 1 persistence item. Another motivation-related factor was extracted also (Factor 14; see later).
2. Tactile–kinesthetic: 4 tactile and 4 kinesthetic items.
3. Set place/set time/mobility: 4 place, 4 mobility, and 2 set-time items. The two set-time items might have been included due to the nature of the items that indicate the need for structure (set) as found in set-place.
4. Audio–visual: 3 auditory and 3 visual items.
5. Light: 4 light and 1 self-motivated. The self-motivated item was not interpretable.
6. Authority figures: 4 authority figures items.
7. Sound: 4 sound items.
8. Alone–peers: 4 alone–peers items.
9. Intake: 4 intake items.

10. Temperature: 4 temperature items.

11. Design: 4 design items.

12. Organizational: 2 set order, 1 structure, 1 set time (this item also loaded on the Factor 3). These items indicate the students' preference for structured homework and for ordering and setting the specific time for homework.

13. Afternoon–evening time: 2 afternoon and 2 evening time items.

14. Motivational 2: 2 responsibility and 2 persistence items.

15. Mobility: 2 mobility items. These two items also loaded on Factor 3.

There were 75 items that loaded on one or more factors with a loading greater than .30. Two motivational factors extracted, with the first factor mostly indicating the source of the motivation (self-, parent-, or teacher-motivated), and the second, consisting of persistence and responsibility. There were 13 of 88 original items that did not significantly load on any of these factors.

In summary, the two morning items may not be good indicators for homework timing because most students are not able to use the morning hours for homework, even if they are inclined to do so. Items that need close examinations are structure, order, set place, and set time that are somehow related to one another in the way they loaded on factors 3 and 12. Other problematic items need to be closely examined to determine whether they should be retained. However, before considering the modification or elimination of the items, internal consistency and item-total correlations were examined.

Internal Consistency Estimates and Item Retention or Elimination Criteria

The internal consistency of the HPQ was assessed with coefficient alpha. For the components with low coefficients, the item-total correlations and item means and dispersions were further examined to detect the problematic items. Additionally, other indices such as factor loadings and item compositions (i.e., consistency and structure of the items) within each component were also considered in selecting items for the next version of the HPQ. The coefficient alpha for each component and the recommendations for the questionnaire revision are presented for each category:

a. Environmental: sound .88, light .83, temperature .81, design .78, place .79. Factor loadings were all greater than .45, and each item loaded on only one factor. All original items were to be retained.

However, a proper category for the set place items needed to be determined.

b. Organizational: structure .39, order .53. One of the four structure items had the item-total correlation of −.06, with a small loading size. An inspection of the four structure items indicated that this one item had a slightly different meaning compared to the other three. One of the four set-order items had the item-total correlation of .16, with a small loading size. Although this item was similar in content with the other three, the sentence was long and rather confusing in wording. An elimination of these two items was considered.

c. Motivational: self-motivated .62, parent-motivated .76, teacher-motivated .49, persistence .67, responsibility .53. The items loaded on two separate factors, both being considered motivational. Although the internal consistency of the responsibility component was relatively low, there was no specific item that caused the low consistency. It was decided that the four items be retained for further examination with another sample. One teacher-motivated item had the item-total correlation of −.02, with a small loading. This item also was badly structured and lengthy, thus we decided to eliminate it.

d. Perceptual-physical: auditory .71, visual .56, tactile .81, kinesthetic .88, intake .82, mobility .76. One auditory and one visual item had the item-total correlation of .10 and .04, respectively, and both had small loadings. The other items were preference about the perceptual mode used by teachers in giving homework instructions. The content of these two questionable items were not closely related to the respective factors, and we decided to eliminate them. The coefficients of the four time-related components were measured separately: set time .47, morning .50, afternoon .55, evening .55. However, all of the time components showed low internal consistencies. Because the specific timing for homework may not be freely chosen by students, the time component may need to be restructured. At this stage, however, we kept all the items for further examination.

e. Sociological: alone–peers .84, authority figures .83. Each item loaded only on one factor, and factor loadings were reasonable. All original items were to be retained.

In summary, we decided that five poor items be eliminated in the next version of the HPQ. We expected that some changes in the arrangement of components needed to occur as well, but we decided not to make the change until we cross-validated these findings with another sample (see Study 3). Additionally, in the interest of increased clarity, two items were revised, one from the light and the other from the temperature component: "I prefer to do my homework in dim light *rather than in bright light;*

I like doing my homework in a cool *rather than in a warm* room" (italics added).

STUDY 3

Overview

The purpose of Study 3 was to further examine the factor structure and internal consistency of the HPQ using another sample. The same grade level (seventh) from another country was used for this purpose. The five items that neither met the psychometric criteria nor had the content consistency of the items within the respective component were deleted for this analyses. However, several questionable items that did not meet some of the retention criteria still remained for further exploratory analyses with the current sample.

Method

The participants were 220 Korean seventh graders (114 males and 106 females). These participants were from six randomly chosen classes from two public junior high schools in the capital of Korea. All students who were present on the day the investigation was conducted participated. The revised HPQ (HPQ-2) was the 83-item questionnaire, which was group administered to students in their classrooms.

Results

Exploratory Factor Analysis

We examined the factor structure with the criteria of 15 factors derived from Study 2 first, with the intention of continuing the analyses in the event that the finding was not deemed appropriate. The 15-factor solution accounted for 51% of the variance. In general, the current findings were consistent with those of Study 2; thus, no further EFA was conducted. The findings are summarized to compare with those of Study 2.

The eigenvalues of the 15 factors ranged from 1.66 to 5.00.

1. Motivational 1: 14 items including 4 self-motivated, 3 teacher-motivated, 1 parent-motivated, 3 persistence, 2 responsibility, 1 structure item.
2. Set place/set time/mobility: 4 set place, 4 mobility, and 1 set-time item.
3. Tactile–kinesthetic: 4 tactile and 4 kinesthetic (same as Study 2).

4. Audio–visual: 3 auditory and 3 visual items (same as Study 2).

5. Temperature: 4 temperature items (same as Study 2).

6. Intake: 4 intake items (same as Study 2).

7. Light: 4 light items.

8. Authority figures: 4 authority figures items (same as Study 2).

9. Sound: 4 sound items (same as Study 2).

10. Design: 4 design items (same as Study 2).

11. Alone–peers: 4 alone–peers items (same as Study 2).

12. Motivational 2: 3 parent-motivated and 2 teacher-motivated. Among these, one parent-motivated and both teacher-motivated items loaded also on Factor 1 (Motivational 1).

13. Kinesthetic: 4 kinesthetic items; all four items also loaded on Factor 3 (tactile–kinesthetic).

14. Organizational: The three set-order items only loaded on this factor, unlike the findings from Study 2, where 2 set order, 1 structure, 1 set time were involved.

15. Evening time: 2 evening items, but without afternoon as found in Study 2.

All together, there were 73 items that loaded on one or more factors with a loading greater than .30. The main differences between the current and previous findings are the items that loaded on motivational factors (Motivational 1 and 2). This time, the first motivational factor was more general including some items from all motivational components, while the second motivational factor consisted of only the source of motivation (parent- and teacher-motivated). These findings and the 10 items that had a loading of smaller than .30 and the internal consistency estimates (later) will be used for further recommendations for the questionnaire revision.

Internal Consistency and Item Selection

The item retention criteria were the same as those used in Study 2. The coefficient alpha and recommendations for the questionnaire revision are as follows:

a. Environmental: sound .82, light .88, temperature .90, design .81, place .72. Factor loadings were all greater than .35 and each item loaded on only one factor. All original items were to be retained.

b. Organizational: structure .65, order .76. With one item eliminated from each component, the internal consistency estimates were improved. Although some of the structure items had relatively small loading sizes, the content of items were consistent. Thus, we retained these items for further examination.

c. Motivational: self-motivated .66, parent-motivated .69, teacher-motivated .78, persistence .58, responsibility .56. The internal consistency estimate of the persistence component in the Korean sample were lower than those of the U.S. sample. However, because of the inconsistency in alpha across the two samples, and the relevance and quality of item composition were reasonable, we decided to retain the four items for further examination.

Two responsibility items in both samples did not load significantly on any factor, whereas the other two were part of items loaded on the motivational factors. Besides, the coefficient alpha was relative low in both samples. Close inspections of the four items indicated that two items regarded the preference to be reminded to do homework, whereas the other two concerned the responsibility to do homework everyday. Thus, it was decided that two additional items be created to further examine the factor structure.

d. Perceptual-physical: auditory .77, visual .71, tactile .88, kinesthetic .88, intake .88, mobility .75. With one auditory and one visual item removed, the internal consistency estimates for all components of this dimension became reasonable.

The coefficients of the four time-related components were: set-time .38, morning .54, afternoon .68, evening .78. Although alpha coefficients for the afternoon and evening were better in this sample than those found in the U.S. sample, the time components, especially the morning, had no discernible loading to any factor in both samples. In light of these findings and because homework time may not be freely chosen by students, the time components have little relevance for homework in the current form and should either be dropped or rewritten to represent the students' preference to use a set or variable time for doing homework.

e. Sociological: alone–peers .83, authority figures .81. Factor loadings were all greater than .45, and each item loaded on only one corresponding factor. All original items were to be retained.

In summary, HPQ-2 with 83 items was to be revised. Two experimental items for responsibility were to be added and the time component items were to be revised to reflect the bipolar preference of set versus variable time of day for doing homework. The two new responsibility items were: "I tend to forget to do my homework" and "I start doing my homework and not finish it." Other items with negligible loadings were not consistent across the two samples, thus will be retained for further examination.

Audio–visual, tactile–kinesthetic, and set place/mobility were extracted as one factor respectively, with some component items (e.g., kinesthetic items) loading on two factors—one that combines the two components and the other with only one of the two. Although these were empirically extracted as one factor, respectively (or two as in kinesthetic), inspections of these items indicate that the items clearly characterize the original respective component. However, one mobility item did not contain characteristic meaning of body "movement," but was closer to changing "place." Further observations needed to be made on the performance of set place and mobility items.

STUDY 4

Overview

The purpose of Study 4 was to examine the factor structure of the HPQ with the samples of students younger (Grade 5) and older (Grades 9 and 10) than those used in the foregoing studies. With the Grade 5 sample, we implemented the change and eliminated the time-element items. With the Grades 9 and 10 samples, we included the two experimental items for the responsibility component. However, the new set-time/variable-time items were not added at this stage. The empirical factor structures from the current and previous studies were compared with the hypothesized five-factor structures to re-examine the appropriateness of structural components in each category of homework motivation and preference.

Method

The participants were 201 fifth graders (104 males, 96 females, and 1 unspecified) from three public elementary school in a large western metropolitan area in the United States. Sixty-three ninth ($n = 24$) and tenth ($n = 39$) graders were used for the analyses of the older student group (24 males and 39 females), who were from three multi-age classes taught by a geometry teacher. These students were from a public school in a western suburban area. Due to the small sample size and to the fact that the students of both grades were taught in a same class, the combination of the two grades was considered acceptable. With the removal of the 8 time-related items, the revised HPQ used with the fifth graders was a 75-item questionnaire (HPQ-3a). The 77-item HPQ-3b was used with the Grades 9 and 10 sample due to the new two additional responsibility items.

Results

*Exploratory Factor Analysis and Internal Consistency in the Grade
5 Sample*

A 13-factor solution, accounting for 46% of the variance, was more
consistent with the findings from Study 2 and 3 than the 14- or 15-factor
solutions. Other solutions with a criterion of a larger or smaller number
of factors did not result in structures that better describe the hypothesized categories and components.

The factor structures were similar to those found in the previous studies just reported, with a slightly better defined structural pattern. The
findings are summarized briefly:

1. Motivational including self-, parent-, and teacher-motivated
   items and one persistent item.

2. Tactile–kinesthetic.

3. Set place/mobility.

4. Intake–design, which included four items each from the two
   respective elements. The loadings were in a bipolar pattern that
   indicated that those who prefer to eat or drink prefer informal
   design of furniture.

5. Auditory–visual.

6. Authority figures.

7. Temperature.

8. Light.

9. Sound.

10. Alone–peers.

11. Organization including all order items as found in Study 3.

12. Motivational, including four responsibility items and two per-
    sistent items, with relatively small-sized loadings.

13. Structure, with four structure items.

Internal consistency estimates ranged from .60 to .84 with an exception
of .59 in the structure component. With the time-related items eliminated
in this study, most items loaded on a factor with a loading greater than
.30. The main differences between this and the previous two factor studies are that the order and structure factors were extracted as two separate
factors, whereas Intake–Design was extracted as one. The small loadings
in the second motivational factor indicate that problems exist in the

responsibility and persistence items, but the findings of the specific items with low loadings were inconsistent across the sample.

Summary of the Findings in the Three Samples

The current and previous two factor analyses indicated the following:

a. The two motivational factors included the original five components (self-, parent-, and teacher-motivated, persistence, and responsibility). One motivational factor included mostly the first three components, which indicated the source of motivation, and the other consisted of two components, which indicated degree of persistence or responsibility of the student, that is, the strength or level of their motivation to do homework. One of the two factors is more inclusive in that some of the items from all five motivational components loaded on this factor. These findings indicate that strong relationships exist among these five motivational components, with stronger relationships among items for the source of motivation and among those for the strength of motivation.

b. Although the set place/variable place and mobility items were extracted as one factor, the mobility component alone was also extracted as a factor (Study 2). Theoretically, the set-place/variable-place component was constructed to determine whether the student prefers a set place or various places for homework in general, whereas mobility was to determine the need for bodily movement regardless of the place preference.

c. In a sample (Study 4), the intake and design components were extracted as one factor, whereas in the other two samples (Studies 2 and 3) they were extracted as two separate factors. With the bipolar pattern of the two components in Study 4 and the findings of Study 2 and 3, these two are considered as two separate components, although they are correlated.

d. Findings varied in the organizational category, with overall consistency of items loading on either of the order or structure component; although in Study 4, items on either component cleanly loaded on the corresponding component only. Two empirical factors contained items from structure, order, set place, set-time components, which can be considered organizational. Except for the set place, these components were originally categorized as organizational; thus it was decided to move the set-place component from the environmental to the organizational category.

e. Other components were extracted as a factor with most items loading only on the corresponding hypothesized factor.

At this point in the validation process, we determined that most of the originally hypothesized five-dimensional structure of homework preferences was to be retained. However, the organizational category would now include structure, set order, and set place. The set-place items assessed whether a student prefers an organized homework setting with a designated place set for homework. The empirical findings and the item content examination led us to make this change. We turn now to results obtained from the older students. It may be recalled that the HPQ used with them in this study included the two experimental items on responsibility.

Exploratory Factor Analysis and Internal Consistency in the Grades 9 and 10 Sample. Because the previous three factor studies resulted in fairly consistent factor structures as provided in the summary of findings just presented, and because the sample size was too small to factor-analyze all the items in their entirety, we examined the factor structure for each category.

(1) Environmental: The four factors extracted matched the four components, sound, light, temperature, and design (accounting for 71% of the variance; coefficient alpha ranging from .87 to .91).

(2) Organizational: Three factors extracted; the first factor (set place) with the original four set-place items loading only on this factor; the second factor (structure) with the three structure items and two order items loading on this factor; the third factor (order) with two order items and one structure item. Thus, the structure and set-order components shared some items. The pattern of correlations suggest that students who preferred structured homework with detailed homework instructions also preferred to organize their assignments according to a certain order. However, the two constructs are conceptually different in that the structure component refers to the nature of the homework assignments themselves, while the order component refers to whether students organize their assignments in a set or variable order (60% of the variance; $\alpha = .75$ to .84).

(3) Motivational: As indicated earlier, we added two responsibility items in this study. All the self-, parent-, and teacher-motivated items loaded on a factor. However, two new and two existing responsibility items and two persistence items also loaded on this factor. The second factor consisted of two existing and one new responsibility items, the latter loading on both first and second factor. These items indicated whether the students prefer to be reminded or have tendency to postpone finishing homework. We decided that the name of this factor needed to be changed to *promptness*, because the items represent more of that disposition than responsibility. The third factor (persistence) consisted of two persistence items and one self-motivation item, with the latter also loading on the first factor.

Thus, the current findings are similar to the previous ones, showing positive correlations among all motivational elements. Although they are empirically correlated, thus representing homework motivation in general, the content of items indicate that distinct components exist. For example, items on the parent-motivated component specifically indicate "parent" as a motivating agent. A close inspection of the two original responsibility items revealed that they more closely measure students' achievement motivation (e.g., "I like to do all my homework each day" and "I do not like to do all my homework each day") than promptness or responsibility. Thus, we decided to eliminate these two items. The new items remained in the questionnaire. With these items, another factor analysis was performed, resulting in structure similar to the above (52% of the variance; $\alpha=.71$ to .88).

(4) Perceptual-physical: The current findings were not different from the previous findings; the audio and visual items loaded on a factor (audio–visual), with a bipolar pattern of audio and visual components. The tactile and kinesthetic items loaded on a factor (tactile–kinesthetic); however, as was indicated in the previous findings, the kinesthetic items by themselves also loaded on another factor (kinesthetic). Although these components were highly related empirically, we considered that they were distinct constructs because items under each component distinctly represent the respective component (e.g., "I prefer to hear the homework instructions from the teacher in class rather than to get them in writing" for auditory). The four mobility items loaded on a factor (mobility), with an exception of an item that also loaded on another factor (intake). The four intake items and the one previously mentioned mobility item loaded on a factor (intake). (65% of the variance; $\alpha=.74$ to .89).

(5) Sociological: A simple two-factor structure was revealed, with the first factor consisting of four alone–peers items and the second four authority figures items (64% of the variance; $\alpha=.83$ to .90).

Overall, the internal consistency estimates (.66 to .91) were higher in this sample than those found with the previous samples with younger students. It is not clear whether the age was the factor causing the difference in the internal consistency estimates, because the findings on the factor structures and coefficient alpha with the fifth-grade sample were similar to or slightly better than those found with the two seventh-grade samples.

Summary of Overall Findings of the Four Studies Discussed So Far. In general, the overall findings from the four samples including U.S. students in Grades 5, 6, 7, and 9 and 10 and seventh graders from Korea provided empirical support for most of the hypothesized factor structure. A few minor modifications were made on the basis of empirical and theoretical considerations.

(1) The set-place component was moved from the environmental to the organizational category. This was based both on a theoretical consideration (i.e., the set-place component is more in line with organizational

dimension) and empirical findings (i.e., the set-place items were part of two extracted factors composed of set-place and other organizational items).

(2) The original time-related items were dropped in the validation process and the new set-time/variable-time items are yet to be included in the organizational category.

(3) We changed the name of a category, environmental, to surroundings. The term *environmental* is more inclusive than *surroundings* because we view that homework environment could include surroundings as well as other categories such as organizational, perceptual-physical, and sociological.

(4) We also changed the name of another category, sociological, to interpersonal at this time. It seemed that the latter describes the category more properly than the former because the category was meant to express how a learner prefers to *inter*-act with another person when doing homework.

(5) As indicated at the onset of the factor-analytic studies, the components under some categories would be factored out as separate components (e.g., environmental components), whereas motivational components would converge into one or two factors due to the expected high correlations among the items. However, the motivational items in each component are conceptually distinct in that they represent the component as indicated with the terms used in each item: for example, "I" for self-motivated, promptness, persistence; "parent" for parent-motivated; "teacher" for teacher-motivated. Throughout the four factor analyses, one of the motivational factors distinctly regarded the *source* of motivation (i.e., self-, parent-, or teacher-motivated), while another indicating the *strength* of the student's homework motivation (i.e., promptness and persistence). Thus, we divided the motivation category into two subcategories to represent the source and strength of motivation. With this change the model now consists of six categories or dimensions.

(6) At the current stage of the validation process, we concluded that the motivation-related constructs were distinctively different from the preference-related constructs. Thus, we rearranged our model to reflect the empirical findings and conceptual foundation, which resulted in two main categories (motivation and preference), with motivation consisting of two subcategories (source and strength) and preferences of four subcategories (organizational, surroundings, perceptual-physical, interpersonal). This model is described in chapter 1.

(7) We also considered that at this time the questionnaire should represent the model, and thus changed the name of the questionnaire (HMPQ) and of the profile (HMPP). Thus, the result of the questionnaire development described thus far is a 75-item questionnaire that taps 20 components of homework preferences that belong to one of the six cat-

egories. In the model we have one more component (time) that we earlier dropped with the intention of modifying and adding new items to reflect set-time/variable-time continuum. Data with these new set of time-related items are currently being collected. However, the previous factor analyses that showed the set-time items loaded on the organizational component justify our reconfiguration of the model with 21 components.

Some of the items still do not show desirable performance consistently across various samples; however, we would recommend against fundamental changes without further consideration of the item comparability on more data. We suggest that although the current HMPQ is not yet the final version it can be used for the purposes of research and educational applications.

STUDY 5

Overview

The purpose of Study 5 was to assess the temporal stability of the HMPQ scores measured over two occasions.

Method

The participants were 329 Chinese fifth graders (172 males and 157 females) in Hong Kong. The students were from a school that housed kindergarten through high school. Both pre- and post-HMPQ were group administered to students in their school classrooms. For the fifth graders, there was a 20-day interval between the two administrations and for the seventh graders a 28-day interval.

Results

The coefficient alpha ranged from .63 to .87 except for two components ($\alpha = .58$ for promptness and $\alpha = .54$ for persistence), with the median internal consistency of .73. The test–retest correlation coefficients ranged from .51 to .82, with the median value of .63. The coefficients for alpha, first, and test–retest correlations, next, are listed here for each component, respectively.

    a. Motivational source—self-motivated: .72, .65; parent-motivated: .70, .61; teacher-motivated: .69, .61.

    b. Motivational strength—promptness: .58, .60; persistence: .54, .60.

    c. Organizational—structure: .64, .51; order: .70, .61; place: .82, .68.

d. Environmental—sound: .84, .82; light: .76, .63; temperature: .76, .60; design: .71, .68.

e. Perceptual-physical—auditory: .63, .54; visual: .64, .56; tactile .76, .68; kinesthetic: .73, .65; intake: .83, .72; mobility: .75, .67.

f. Interpersonal—alone–peers: .80, .62; authority figures: .87, .65.

The test–retest correlation coefficients were expected to be lower than the coefficient alpha. However, some of the reliability estimates were lower than desired, whereas others exhibited the desired levels of reliability. Increasing item numbers for each component may be one of the solutions that can be considered. However, participants in this and previous studies have reported the questionnaire to be exhaustingly lengthy and their inclination to become careless toward the end of the questionnaire. Nevertheless, the reliability, especially the temporal stability, should be further studied.

STUDY 6

Overview

The purpose of Study 6 was to determine the construct validity of the HMPQ by examining homework motivation and preference scores of each HMPQ component in students who reported themselves to be high or low homework achievers. We predicted that some of the HMPQ scores would be different for groups of high versus low-achieving students, whereas others would not. It has been found that the level of motivation and school achievement are highly related (e.g., Bandura, 1993; Pajares, 1996; Schunk, 1991). Accordingly, it was predicted that the high achievers would report higher scores than would low achievers on the homework motivation components. Evidence of perceptual sensitivity difference between these groups have been rarely reported; that is, perceptual strengths (auditory, visual, tactile, kinesthetic) indicate individual preferences of the way students learn, and not one component of perceptual modalities can definitely distinguish high or low achievers. Thus, the group differences in the HMPQ score (but no differences in some components) in the predicted directions would be an evidence of construct validity of the HMPQ scores.

Method

The participants were 272 seventh-graders (134 males and 138 females) from a public middle school in a large western metropolitan area. The HMPQ was group administered to students in their school classrooms.

Homework achievement as perceived by the students themselves was used for grouping the high and low homework achievers. In addition to the HMPQ data collection, four items that assessed participants' self-perception of their homework achievement were administered. Participants rated on a 5-point scale indicating the degree of agreement. Examples of the items were "If grades were given for homework, I would get a high grade" and "I finish the homework that is assigned to me every time." The internal consistency of the perceived homework achievement was .78.

For all analyses of group differences, those who scored higher than approximately 66th percentile were considered as high achievers, those who scored lower than approximately 33th percentile as low achievers, and those who scored in between as medium level of achievers. A multivariate analysis of variance (MANOVA) was performed followed by univariate analyses of variances (ANOVA) to determine the achievement-group differences on the overall HMPP score and on the individual component scores, respectively.

Results

A statistically significant group difference was found in MANOVA, $p < .0005$, with a relatively strong association between the group difference and the overall HMPP score, $\eta^2 = .41$. Follow-up univariate ANOVAs indicated ten of the 20 elements of preferred homework style distinguished the three levels of self-perceived homework achievement. They were self-, parent-, and teacher-motivated, promptness, persistence, structure, order, light, $ps < .001$, and alone–peers and authority figures, $ps < .02$.

Students who perceived their homework achievement high were motivated by all sources of motivation including self, parent, and teachers, and their strength of homework motivation was reflected by their high promptness and persistent scores, compared to their peers. High homework achievers also preferred structured homework, liked to organize homework in a certain order, and preferred to work in a brightly illuminated home environment and to work alone not with peers but with adult figures, when compared to their peers.

Thus, students who represent different levels of homework achievement showed differences in all motivational, some of the organizational, and all interpersonal components, thus providing additional evidence for the construct validity of the HMPQ. As predicted, none of the perceptual components and most of the environmental components did not distinguish between the high and low achievement groups, indicating that within-group differences were larger than between-group differences in these components. These findings show that there is no particular perceptual channel or particular environment (except for light in this sample) that is strongly related to achievement level, and students of any level of achievement may prefer to work through certain perceptual modes and in certain environments. In other studies (Hong & Lee, 1999b) with Chinese students, most environmental elements (except temperature) and physical element (food intake and mobility) also distinguished high and low self-perceived homework achievers. The differences between the two studies may be cultural- or sample-specific. However, these studies in general provide the construct validity evidence of the HMPQ by showing differences in homework motivation and no differences in perceptual modalities among various levels of homework achievement groups.

STUDY 7

Overview

Study 7 examined the concurrent validity of the HMPQ. The concurrent validity was investigated within each category of the HMPQ by examining the correlations among the components of the particular category. That is, each component score as well as intercorrelations among them were measured and computed concurrently. The components of some of the categories of the HMPQ were not expected to correlate highly. For example, temperature would not be related significantly to other environmental components because it is a distinct entity; that is, preferring a warm or cool temperature would not have a significant relationship to preferring a bright or dim light. However, some of the other components were predicted to be highly correlated. For instance, all motivational components represent motivation, thus expecting high intercorrelations. Although one might predict auditory–visual, tactile–kinesthetic, and intake–mobility preferences to be related to each other, there may not be significant relational patterns showing audio–visual preference associated with tactile or kinesthetic element. This correlational study is not very different from the exploratory factor analyses described earlier because both are based on item intercorrelations. However, Study 7 provides more specific information for each component.

Method

The participants for the concurrent validity study were those described in Study 5. Briefly, they were 329 Chinese fifth graders (172 males and 157 females) in Hong Kong. In this study, the first measure of HMPQ

Table 2.1
Intercorrelations among the Motivational Elements

	Self-motivated	Parent-motivated	Teacher-motivated	Persistence
Parent-motivated	.56*			
Teacher-motivated	.59*	.58*		
Persistence	.39*	.24*	.26*	
Promptness	.58*	.34*	.40*	.31*

* p < .0005.

was used. The correlation coefficients with larger than .20 with the .0005 level of significance were considered as showing a significant relationship due to the large sample size used in the analyses.

Results: Concurrent Validity Evidence

(1) Motivational subscales. We provided the intercorrelations among the components of two subcategories of motivation dimension (source and strength) in Table 2.1. The five motivational components were highly correlated with each other. As expected, students who were self-motivated were also parent- and teacher-motivated as well as persistent and responsible in doing their homework. Other intercorrelations of these concurrent measures were also high in a predictable manner that demonstrates a fair degree of concurrent validity.

(2) Organizational subscales. Among the three organizational components (structure, order, place), order had significant, positive relationships with structure ($r = .22$) and set-place ($r = .26$), $ps < .0005$. These predictable relationships indicate that individuals who preferred structured homework instructions and assignments also preferred to organize the assignments according to a certain order, which can bring a structure to their homework situations. These students also preferred to do homework in the same place in the home, showing again a preference to a structured homework situation. However, a preference to the structured homework instructions did not have a significant relationship with the preference in using the same or different places in the home ($r = .14$). There were no new time-related items at this time of data collection.

(3) Surroundings subscales. Table 2.2 presents the intercorrelations among the surroundings components. The pattern of the correlations indicate that students who prefer a quiet home environment when doing their homework prefer more light and a formal design (desk and chair). The students who prefer a well-lit room also preferred a formal design.

Table 2.2
Intercorrelations among the Environmental Elements

	Sound	Light	Temperature
Light	-.25*		
Temperature	-.15	.12	
Design	-.34*	.23*	.05

* $p < .0005$.

Formal design preference is closely related to preferences to more light and quiet environment in a predictable manner. However, temperature did not show any discernible relationships with other environmental elements.

(4) Perceptual-physical subscales. Again, the pattern of intercorrelations among the perceptual-physical components revealed the predictable relationships (Table 2.3). One of the reasons for the negative correlation between auditory and visual preferences might be that some of the items for these elements compared the auditory and visual preferences (e.g., "I prefer that the homework instructions be given orally and not in writing."). Both tactile and kinesthetic elements involve certain body parts (hands or the whole body), which lead to experiential learning. For example, homework assignments involving actual experience (kinesthetic) could be tactile because a particular actual experience can require a tactual mode of learning.

Students who prefer to eat or drink while doing homework would have a tendency to move about because the eating behavior itself or the process of getting food causes body movements, thus expecting the positive relationship. All the other intercorrelations were not significant (discriminant). Again, these concurrent measures of correlation coefficients between component subscales revealed the predictable pattern of relationships providing more evidence for the validity of the HMPQ scores.

(5) Interpersonal. The relationship between the two components—alone–peers and authority figures—was weak ($r = .15$) and not significant at the .0005 level, indicating that the student's preference to work with peers may not have a close relationship with their preference to have adults around when doing their homework. That is, students who enjoy working with friends do not necessarily like adult supervision. The relationship of these elements may be those that show more strong cultural and developmental impacts that need further examination.

In summary, the findings of the correlation coefficients between the component subscales ranged from predictably low to predictably high. These correlations, especially those that measured the similar constructs

Table 2.3
Intercorrelations among the Perceptual-Physical Elements

	Auditory	Visual	Tactile	Kinesthetic	Intake
Visual	-.39*				
Tactile	.06	.05			
Kinesthetic	.07	-.08	.36*		
Intake	.07	-.02	.03	-.03	
Mobility	.05	-.12	.02	-.07	.39*

* $p < .0005$.

within dimensions (e.g., motivational and organizational elements), are indices of concurrent validity of the subscales within the respective dimension. We did not expect all subscale intercorrelations to have high correlations and they should not because some of the components within a certain dimension represent a distinctly different construct. In general, the predictable pattern of correlation coefficients shown between component subscales indicates a reasonable degree of concurrent validity of the HMPQ scores. Although Study 7 was not intended to provide major discriminant validity evidence, a glimpse of it was evident in the findings of the predicted low correlation patterns between some components. Study 8 provided further evidence on the discriminant validity.

STUDY 8

Overview

Study 8 examined the construct validity of the HMPQ by examining the discriminant validity of the instrument. The discriminant validity was determined by investigating whether the HMPQ can discriminate between the individuals who are characterized as highly talented in science, social leadership, and dance. The three areas were chosen due to the clear differences in activities and creative quality involved in each. It was predicted that although certain components of the HMPQ would differentiate students in one talent area, others would differentiate those in other talent areas. For example, students who are highly active in social leadership may like to study with peers when doing homework, whereas those who are talented in the dance area may prefer to move about when doing homework. Although there has not been a study examining these relationships, we predict some distinguishing pattern of relationships would emerge in this exploration. The HMPQ's capacity to discriminate these individuals through its differentiating components would provide further evidence for the construct validity, specifically discriminant validity.

Method

The participants for this study were 126 fifth graders from Israel (48 boys, 76 girls, and 1 unspecified). Student talents in science, leadership, and dance are assessed by the Tel-Aviv Activities and Accomplishments Inventory (TAAI; Milgram, 1998) that measured out-of-school activities and accomplishments. Thirteen items tapped the science domain, 12 the social leadership, and 10 the dance area. Examples of such accomplishments include receiving an award for a science project, being chosen for a leadership position in a youth group, and giving a solo dance performance. Subjects indicated their out-of-school activities and accomplishments by answering yes or no to each item. Both HMPQ and TAAI were group administered in school classrooms at the same time with no time limits.

The construct validity of the TAAI including discriminant, predictive, and factorial validity have been evidenced in various studies (e.g., Hong & Milgram, 1996; Hong, Milgram, & Gorsky, 1995; Hong, Milgram, & Whiston, 1993; Hong, Whiston, & Milgram, 1993; Milgram & Hong, 1994; Milgram & Milgram, 1976).

Results: Discriminant Validity Evidence

The activities and accomplishment scores in science, social leadership, and dance were correlated with the HMPQ component scores. Table 2.4 presents the HMPQ components that showed significant relationships with the scores in the three talent areas. As predicted, some components were only distinctly related to talents of some domains but not to other domains; hence the discriminant validity evidence. The preference of organizing homework assignments was highly related only to the science-talented youths, whereas the students talented in the dance domain preferred to move about and also changed places in the home when doing their homework. The pattern is predictable in that individuals who practice dancing would likely be engaged in bodily movements. By the same token, the students with leadership talents reported the preference to do their homework with peers, which was also predictable. Science-talented individuals were self-, parent-, and teacher-motivated in doing homework, whereas those students who show social leadership were more parent- and teacher-motivated and persistent. However, those talented in dance were not particularly motivated in doing homework.

These findings do not depart from our expectations. The talented in science tend to be high academic achievers in that subject area, and most

Table 2.4

Correlations between the HMPQ Element Scores and Activities or Accomplishment Scores in Science, Social Leadership, and Dance

	Science	Leadership	Dance
Motivational			
Self-motivated	.26**		
Parent-motivated	.30**	.19*	
Teacher-motivated	.28**	.35***	
Persistence		.20*	
Promptness			
Organizational			
Structure			
Order	.19*		
Place		-.22*	-.25*
Perceptual-physical			
Auditory	.18*	.20*	
Visual			.19*
Tactile	.32***	.38***	.20*
Kinesthetic	.38***		
Intake			
Mobility			.19*
Interpersonal			
Alone/peers		.20*	
Authority figures			

Note. None of the surroundings components had a significant relationship with talent activities, thus removed from the table. Only those correlation coefficients significant at least at the .05 level were reported.
* $p < .05$. ** $p < .005$. *** $p < .0005$.

accomplishments in science outside of school are based on the knowledge they acquired in their in-school science courses. Students' interest in science is encouraged and supported by their teachers or their parents (see chapter 6 on the gifted and talented). Therefore, the motivation coming from all three sources is understandable. That the talented in social leadership were parent- and teacher-motivated is not surprising because of their tendency to strive to satisfy the people around them. That the talented in dance did not show high motivation is again understandable because homework assignments are not likely in the dance area.

Some of the perceptual components distinguished the talented in some areas. This is a highly interesting finding. In the previous research with academic achievement (also see chapter 5), the perceptual components did not distinguish the high versus low academic achievers. However, with the talented students, the outcome was different. The tactile component seems to be influential in all three areas studied; students who were talented in science, leadership, and dance preferred to learn through the tactile mode. That the talented in science and social leadership preferred to learn via auditory channel, whereas the dance-talented preferred a visual channel also indicates that the HMPQ components discriminate the talented in various domains. Although the science-talented preferring the auditory learning is not easily interpretable, the social leaders preferring to learn by talking and listening and dancers by seeing do not challenge the common theoretical senses.

In summary, the pattern of relationships in each talent supports our contention that the HMPQ components have the capacity to discriminate talents in different domains, thus providing additional construct validity evidence.

STUDY 9

Overview

Because the HMPQ assesses various aspects of the ways students prefer to study at home as well as their motivation source and strength, it is quite a lengthy questionnaire for school children. The negative feedback received from the participating teachers and students regarding the HMPQ has been mostly on the length of the questionnaire. Although the use of class time has been an issue due to the length of the questionnaire, the most disturbing feedback was that some students grew tired of responding to the items and became careless when they reached the end of the questionnaire.

The first version of the HMPQ was an 88-item questionnaire. During the validation process, some items were revised, eliminated, and substituted, and thus the HMPQ became a 75-item instrument. These 75 items tap the 20 components of homework motivation and preference profile, with each component consisting of four items except for a few components with three items due to the elimination of poor items.

With the feedback on the length and the imbalance on the number of items per component, we decided to test a short form of the HMPQ. Although we realize that shortening the questionnaire would compromise the psychometric quality of the instrument, an examination of a new data set collected with the short form was needed to determine whether use of this form would enhance student attitudes about completing the questionnaire and whether the short form would indeed compromise the quality of the questionnaire. The internal consistency and temporal stability of the brief form were examined in this study.

Method

The participants were 234 Grade 5 students (114 boys and 120 girls) from two elementary schools in the capital of Korea. All students who were present on the day the investigation was conducted participated. The HMPQ short form was administered twice within a 2-week interval between the two administrations. Only those students with complete data on both pre- and post-HMPQ were included in the 234 database.

Development of the HMPQ: Brief Form

The internal consistency estimates and item-total correlations for each element were collected throughout the validation process for various samples already mentioned. The worst behaving item of the four items in each component was identified and removed from the HMPQ. This procedure resulted in 60 items tapping the 20 components of homework motivation and preference, thus each component consisted of three items (the time items were not included in this form). The poor item identified in most components was consistent across the samples we examined previously. For the poor items identified inconsistently from sample to sample, the content of the items was carefully reviewed again for selecting one worst item to be removed.

Results: Internal Consistency and Test–Retest Reliability

The coefficient alpha for pre- and post-HMPQ and temporal stability (test–retest reliability) for scores based on the HMPQ brief form are presented in Table 2.5.

Although we expected somewhat lower internal consistency estimates due to shortening the questionnaire, the reliability estimates were as good as or in some cases better than those found with the original long form. It is speculated that due to the reasonable length of the questionnaire, more students in this study than those in previous studies responded with sincerity up to the last item, resulting in comparable or even better consistency.

As indicated in Table 2.5, internal consistency estimates ranged from .61 to .90 in the pre-HMPQ scores and from .61 to .91 in the post-HMPQ scores. The temporal stability indicated by correlation coefficients between the two administrations of the same questionnaire ranged from .65 to .84, which is considered quite acceptable. With these results, we conclude that the HMPQ brief form can be utilized for research and also for diagnostic and intervention purposes by school teachers and parents.

Table 2.5
Internal Consistency and Test–Retest Reliability for Pre- and Post-HMPQ Short Form Scores

Homework style element	Coefficient α		Test-retest reliability
	Pre-HPQ	Post-HPQ	
Motivational			
Self-motivated	.76	.83	.76
Parent-motivated	.70	.79	.79
Teacher-motivated	.69	.78	.76
Persistence	.64	.62	.70
Responsibility	.62	.61	.73
Organizational			
Structure	.61	.69	.65
Order	.70	.82	.68
Place	.71	.76	.65
Surroundings			
Sound	.76	.78	.81
Light	.84	.89	.70
Temperature	.90	.90	.77
Design	.70	.65	.75
Perceptual-Physical			
Auditory	.66	.77	.67
Visual	.75	.80	.67
Tactile	.87	.91	.84
Kinesthetic	.83	.86	.80
Intake	.75	.79	.73
Mobility	.73	.75	.79
Individual/Social			
Alone-peers	.74	.78	.74
Authority figures	.80	.79	.72

Note. N = 234.

GENERAL DISCUSSION

The findings in these studies provide evidence that the HMPQ can be used as a tool for determining the homework motivation and preference of school-aged children. The various samples tested differed in age and country of residence, but the findings obtained with these samples were fairly consistent. The HMPQ demonstrated a reasonable degree of stable factor structure as well as of temporal stability and internal consistency. The construct validity evidence of the HMPQ scores including concurrent and discriminant validity and the analysis of achievement-group differences added to the justification for using the instrument with children. The empirical findings that resulted from the validation process also contributed to the development of a conceptual model of homework motivation and preference.

On the basis of the factor analyses and findings of internal consistency used for item refinement and elimination, we concluded that the content validity of the instrument is adequate. Additionally, it was a rather pleasant surprise to see that on some psychometric indicators of reliability the brief form of HMPQ performed as well as or even better than the HMPQ long form. Thus, the brief form may be regarded as a reasonably reliable and valid instrument to be used as an alternative to or perhaps in place of the long form. The shorter instrument can be useful in future research on homework, in general, and especially on studies of the efficacy of intervention programs using the children's homework motivation and preference profiles in the effort to improve student homework behavior.

Although these studies provide evidence for the HMPQ reliability, validity, and usefulness, some of the components showed lower reliability than desired, indicating that continuing improvement and refinement in the content of items is necessary before the instrument can be presented commercially. For example, items that measure preference for changing bodily position by physically squirming or moving around from place to place and the preference for doing homework in the same or in various places are clearly distinct conceptually but not empirically. The existence of this problem became apparent as a result of the factor analyses, where in some cases component scores on mobility and place were extracted as one factor, and in others, as separate factors.

Studies with children younger than Grade 5 have not been conducted. Accordingly, the suitability of the HMPQ with younger students and with older age groups not yet studied, remain to be examined. Revisions of the instrument should continue on an ongoing basis until representative samples of groups who differ in age, and other individual difference dimensions are examined.

Recently the LSI (Dunn et al., 1987) has received negative evaluations on its validity. Hughes (1992), Kavale, Hirshoren, and Forness (1998), and Westman (1992) pointed out that the LSI does not pay sufficient attention to issues of construct validity and that theoretical development has been limited. Moreover, published data on the LSI does not include information on the relationship of the subscales or on the relationship between the psychometric factor structure and the theoretical framework. They further indicated that reports of low internal consistency and the absence of test–retest reliability make it difficult to justify making instructional decisions based on the LSI. Because the learning style formulations and measures provided the initial impetus for our work, the recent wave of criticism was of concern. Our current conceptualization of homework performance and the HMPQ developed to assess it is distinct from the original learning style concept and measure in many ways, as explained in chapter 1 and in this chapter as well. Our measure should be evaluated on the basis of the psychometric evidence presented in the current chapter and in future development.

PART II

RESEARCH ON HOMEWORK MOTIVATION AND PREFERENCE

3

Preferred versus Actual and Parental Awareness of Homework Performance

The way students prefer to do their homework and the conditions under which they actually do it in their homes may or may not be the same. In this chapter, we first examine preferred–actual gaps in homework motivation and preferences and discuss the similarities and differences between preferred versus actual homework performance. The cause of the preferred–actual gap may be that parents are unaware of their children's personal preferences about when, where, and how to do homework. We continue first by presenting what has been found on the question of the degree of parental awareness of their children's homework motivation and preferences, and then by examining what is known about the degree to which parents are likely to permit children to do homework according to their preferences. Finally, we suggest why increasing parent awareness of their children's homework preferences and their willingness to accommodate them should be assigned top priority in the work of teachers and counselors. The effects of preferred–actual gaps on homework achievement are discussed in chapter 5.

SIMILARITIES AND DIFFERENCES BETWEEN PREFERRED AND ACTUAL HOMEWORK PERFORMANCE

When learning in school or when doing homework, learners are not always permitted to learn under preferred conditions. Teachers and parents frequently have strong views about which learning conditions will produce the best academic results and these views may be in strong contrast to the learner's preferred conditions. The actual conditions under which a person learns, as determined in school by the teacher and at home by the parent, may not always match the learner's individual preferences. In light of findings that clearly demonstrate increased academic achievement and more positive attitudes toward school when the way children prefer to learn and the way they actually learn were matched, the existence of a preferred–actual learning style gap is unfortunate.

In school settings, the teacher usually determines the conditions under which learning occurs. Because the learner's choices are limited, a large discrepancy between preferred and actual ways of studying is understandable. At home, however, one might assume that because the learner determines to a much greater extent the conditions under which he or she learns, there will be little if any discrepancy between preferred and actual ways of at-home learning. This reasonable assumption, however, should be investigated empirically. Therefore, we first proposed a conceptual distinction between preferred and actual style of performing homework tasks and investigated whether a gap existed between them.

We compared preferred and actual source and strength of motivation and preference in the organizational, surroundings, perceptual-physical, and interpersonal categories (Hong & Milgram, 1999). We administered two questionnaires, the HPQ and the Homework Questionnaire (HQ), that assessed preferred and actual homework performance, respectively. These instruments were five-point Likert scales, with the mean score 1 indicating *strongly disagree*, 2 *disagree*, 3 *uncertain*, 4 *agree*, and 5 *strongly agree* for each component examined. This study used the HPQ that was not yet modified to HMPQ (see chapter 2). Thus, responsibility items (of motivation category) were the original four items that have not been changed to the four promptness items. The two questionnaires were the same in the number and content of items, and in the names and number of component scores. The difference between the two questionnaires was the verb used. In the HPQ "prefer to" or "like to" was used in the items, whereas in the HQ "do," or verbs that describe what they actually do (e.g., "finish," "sit"), were used.

A MANOVA was performed to compare the preferred–actual homework scores of 272 U.S. seventh-grade students. Overall there was a statistically significant difference between the preferred and actual ways of doing homework, $p < .0005$. Follow-up correlation analyses and univariate analyses on each component of the preferred and actual homework performance revealed interesting data on students' homework motivation and preference profiles. Preferred–actual correlation coefficients ranged from .35 to .77. There was no component with a correlation coefficient larger than .80, but there were many with moderate to strong correlations. These findings indicate that although students' preferred and actual homework performance showed some similarity, there were differences between how they prefer to do their homework and how they actually do it. Similarities and differences of the preferred and actual homework performance are discussed below. The mean component scores for statistically significant preferred–actual differences are presented.

Motivational Source and Strength

Preferred and actual scores on the motivational components were moderately related (correlations from .59 to .65), except for a weak preferred–actual correlation (.35) for the responsibility score. In general, motivation levels of all components in this category were fairly high (all mean scores were larger than 3).

Overall, students' motivation to do well in doing homework was relatively high, although they reported that they preferred to be more self-motivated (4.14) than they actually were (3.81). This applies to persistence also; although students preferred to finish all homework assignments even if they are difficult (3.63), they actually did so to a lesser degree (3.48) than they like. The preferred and actual responsibility elements were neither highly consistent nor significantly different from each other. Although some students might have wanted to be responsible for their own homework, many actually did not follow their will; however, the pattern was not consistent as indicated by the low correlation.

Although students reported that they liked to do their homework to satisfy parents or teachers (3.73 and 3.79, respectively), when they reported their actual behavior, the level of parent- or teacher-motivated homework was lower than they preferred it to be (3.60 for both). Overall, more students wanted to and actually do their homework well to satisfy parents and teachers, although some students commented that they do their work for themselves but not to please others; these students represented a minority in the classes tested.

The intercorrelations among these motivational components ranged from .36 to .65. In both preferred and actual measures, highly self-motivated students were more persistent, responsible, and parent- and teacher-motivated, and vice versa, except for the responsibility component of the preference measure with the parent- and teacher-motivated elements. That is, although students who were actually motivated by parents or teachers did report having a higher level of responsibility than those who were not, these relationships with the preference measures were very weak. The findings regarding the relationships of responsibility should be interpreted with caution due to the low internal consistency.

Organizational Preference

Preferred–actual correlation coefficients for structure (.42), order (.55), and place (.67) ranged from low to moderate, indicating both similarities and differences between the preferred and actual organizational homework behaviors. Some students' preferences were met with their actual way of doing homework to a high degree, whereas some were met to a low degree.

Structural preferences (3.76), whether they like to get detailed and exact homework instructions from teachers, were not significantly different from whether they actually do better with the actual homework structure they were receiving from the teachers (3.72). Although the mean preference and actual scores did not differ and more students wanted structured than general instructions from teachers, there seems to be less than desirable agreement between preferred–actual structure ($r = .42$). Classroom teachers should be cognizant about students' preferences and should try to accommodate these preferences to the best of their ability.

Although students have a tendency to prefer to (3.48) and actually organize homework assignments in a certain order (3.30), more students reported they did not actually organize as much as they prefer to do. Moderate degree of consistency was found in the use of a set place or variable places in the home. Overall, their preferred (2.87) and actual (2.93) ways of choosing places were not significantly different and there was a tendency for an uncertainty in their preferences toward the use of one or different places when studying at home.

Surroundings Preference

The components with strong preferred–actual relationships were all from the surroundings category ($rs < .70$), except for temperature. Students who preferred certain levels of background sound and light to some degree actually did their homework with the conditions of their preferences. However, a mean comparison between preferred and actual measures on the sound component indicated that overall more students reported that background sounds were present during real home study conditions (3.47) more often than they preferred (3.37). On the light component, more students preferred to study with bright lights (3.69) than actually did so (3.54). However, the overall mean of around 3.6 indicates that the students from this U.S. sample did not particularly prefer either bright or dim lighting, but studied with a slightly brighter light.

In general, students preferred to and actually did study in an informal design of furniture, for example, lying on a carpet or bed, or reclining in an easy chair (means smaller than 3). However, more students reported a preference for studying in informal seating (2.41) than actually doing homework in that way (2.62). That is, although some of these students preferred an informal design of furniture, they actually studied while sitting at a traditional desk and chair (formal design).

As mentioned earlier, the one surroundings component that had low preferred–actual relationship was temperature. Students reporting their certain preferences to cool or warm temperature did not consistently perform their homework according to their preferences. Overall, the degrees of preferred and actual level of temperature were not significantly different, both 2.90, close to the level of uncertainty in their preferences regarding the room temperature.

Perceptual–Physical Preference

The components of perceptual and physical category were somewhat consistent across the preferred and actual observations of students' own homework modes, as indicated by the moderate correlations between the two constructs that ranged from .51 to .70. Therefore, some students who preferred to do their homework using their certain strong perceptual modalities actually did so, whereas others did not.

Students both preferred and actually did receive homework instructions orally (3.82 and 3.53 for preferred and actual, respectively) rather than did visually (2.46 and 2.80, respectively), with low to moderate consistency between preferred and actual measures in both auditory (.53) and visual (.51) elements. We are unable to expound on these results as to whether the actual way of receiving homework instructions in class habituated students to prefer to get them in that way (i.e., more auditory than visual), or if this is a tendency that seventh graders show. However, this apparent difference between the two modality preferences in homework instructions defies the previous findings in in-school learning styles. Barbe and Milone (1981) suggested primary grade children tend to be more auditory than visual because their interaction with others primarily depends on speaking and listening; and the visual and kinesthetic modalities become more dominant between late elementary grade students and adulthood as students are expected to read and write more frequently. Price, Dunn, and Sanders (1980), however, found that very young children are the most tactile or kinesthetic, that there is a gradual development of visual strengths throughout the elementary grade years, and that not until fifth or sixth grade can most youngsters learn and retain information through the auditory sense. Our results were more in line with the latter authors indicating that by seventh grade, students may be more accustomed to hearing teachers, thus they become more auditory in learning.

Another speculation on the discrepancy among these previous and current studies comes from whether the instructions are for in-class teaching or for homework assignments. It might be that students preferred to and actually did hear more in order to clearly understand the instructions. With the auditory component, the students preferred to hear the instructions more than they actually did hear them, whereas in visual, they actually see the homework instructions more often than they preferred to see them. These findings indicate that teachers need to give homework instructions with clear oral explanations in addition to the visual instructions, in order to help students understand them.

Students reported that they prefer to do homework assignments that require them to use their hands (tactile; 3.24) more than they actually do (3.06). However, no difference between the preferred and actual use of kinesthetic modality was found. On average, students did not show particular perceptual preferences in either tactile or kinesthetic elements, indicated by the mean scores around 3.

The high moderate level of relationship between preferred and actual measures of intake (.66) and mobility (.61) indicate that many of those who preferred to eat or move about while doing homework actually did so. The mean intake scores showed that more students preferred to (3.56) and actually (3.22) do eat or drink while doing homework than not, although they did not actually do so as much as they liked. The mean scores of the preferred (2.84) and actual mobility need (2.97) indicated that although in general students did not express strong preferences in either direction for body movement while doing homework, more students preferred not to move around than they actually did. Although some of these students might have considered that completing homework without moving about would be more effective, their body did not follow their mind as they hoped.

The intercorrelations among the perceptual-physical components of both preferred and actual measures resulted in expected directions and magnitudes. The auditory and visual elements were negatively related (−.75 and −.63, for preferred and actual measures, respectively), indicating that auditory students were less visual and vice versa. Tactile and kinesthetic were positively related (.68 and .82, for preferred and actual, respectively), suggesting that hands-on learning and experiential learning are viewed in a similar way. Some students who liked to or actually ate or drank also moved about while doing homework (.30 and .35, for preferred and actual, respectively).

Interpersonal Preference

Moderate degree of consistency existed between the preferred and actual measures in the components of this category (.58 and .65, for the alone–peers and authority figures component, respectively). Although in general students did not have a strong preference either to work alone or with peers (2.99), they worked alone (2.65) more than they actually preferred to do so. Overall, a tendency was revealed toward not wanting adults around (2.50) and also actually not having them around (2.69) when students did their homework. The two mean scores indicated that some of the students who preferred not to have adults around actually had them while doing homework. This situation may occur because parents want to play a supervisory role in their children's lives. However, the mean actual score of the authority figure component was only 2.69, suggesting that the degree of parental supervision is not as high. There was no discernible relationship between the alone–peers and authority figure elements: Preferring to study alone or with peers is not significantly related to whether students want to have adult figures around when doing homework.

Conclusions

We found that the students' preferred and actual ways of doing homework are conceptually and empirically distinguishable. The preferred–actual distinction represents a contribution to the learning style knowledge base. The data indicated that although some students actually do their homework in their preferred ways, many others experience a gap between what they prefer and what they actually do. The practical implication of the findings are that strenuous efforts should be made by teachers and parents to eliminate or at least to decrease the preferred–actual gap.

Just as many learners do not learn in school according to their individual preferences, many do not do their homework as they would prefer either. The fact that learning is taking place at home is, therefore, no guarantee that individuals will learn using their preferred modes. The reason is probably because parents or other home circumstances, but not the children themselves, determine the conditions for learning at home. The gap between preferred and actual homework performance motivation and preference may be due to parents who are aware of children's preferences but who are not willing to allow them to do their homework in their preferred ways or it may be the result of a parental lack of awareness of learner's preferences.

PARENTAL AWARENESS OF HOMEWORK

We examined the degree of parental awareness of children's homework performance motivation and preference. The results of our studies of parental awareness of children's homework preferences are reported here. These data provided an indication of whether it is reasonable to attribute the preferred–actual gap in homework performance to lack of parent awareness.

Parental Awareness of Children's Homework Motivation and Preference

Most parents care for their children and want to be involved in all aspects of their development including homework activities (Epstein & Sanders, 1998). Most parents structure home life and create a home environment that influences how children do homework. In a study on parent involvement with children's schooling, about half of the parents reported daily involvement with homework (Smock & McCormick, 1995). Parental involvement in homework is not an unadulterated blessing. It can be a double-edged sword, either positive in its influence or destructive and damaging to academic achievement and attitudes and a source of conflict between parents and children (Perkins & Milgram 1996). One reason why parental involvement may contribute negatively is that parents may not be sufficiently aware of children's preferences for conditions under which they prefer to do their homework.

Research on parental involvement as a factor in the homework process, in general, is in itself sparse (Cooper, 1989b). Although researchers have suggested the importance of parental involvement in the homework process, the level of parental awareness of children's homework behavior and preferred homework style rarely have been investigated. Hoover-Dempsey, Bassler, and Burow (1995), in their research on homework as the most common point of intersection among parent, child, and school activities, revealed information about parents' thinking, strategies, and actions related to homework (e.g., concern for a child's unique characteristics as balanced with school demands, questions about appropriate levels of independent work, efforts to structure homework activities, direct involvement in homework tasks). Parents often felt ill-prepared about homework tasks by limitations in knowledge and competing demands for their time and energy. One strategy that could help parents prepare to assist children in doing their homework is to be cognizant of their children's preferred homework style and homework behavior. Once parents are aware of them, they can help children by accommodating home environment to match their children's preferred way of doing homework.

DeBello and Guez (1996) asked parents of fourth- through sixth-grade students to describe how their children learn best, based on the emotional, sociological, physiological, and environmental elements of the LSI (Dunn et al., 1987). Findings indicated no significant correlations between parental perceptions of a child's learning style and the child's own responses. By contrast, parental awareness of child's preferred learning modes and conditions were reasonably accurate in some studies (e.g., Hong & Lee, 1999a; Hong, Milgram, & Perkins, 1995; Perkins & Milgram, 1996). The Hong and Lee investigated the degree of parental awareness of children's homework motivation and preference and its effects on homework and academic achievement and homework attitude in 329 Chinese fifth graders (172 boys and 157 girls) and 244 seventh graders (130 boys and 114 girls) and their parents. They found parental awareness of children's homework motivation and preference fairly accurate in some parents. Moreover, a higher level of parental awareness of child's homework preferences was associated with a child having both higher achievement and more positive attitudes toward homework.

Hong, Milgram, and Perkins (1995) compared the level of parental awareness between Korean and U.S. parents. Korean parents reported higher levels of awareness of their children's homework motivation and preference and understood some components of their children's preferences that are highly important in determining the efficacy of homework behavior. For example, Korean parents understood a child's need for appropriate lighting, an aspect of the learning environment that parents can easily adjust for children. Hong, Milgram, and Perkins (1995) and Perkins and Milgram (1996) investigated the degree to which parents understand their children's in-school and out-of-school learning style preferences. The effects of parental understanding on the attitude toward homework and on homework achievement of children were also examined. In both studies it was found that parents, as a group, had a relatively accurate understanding of the conditions under which their children prefer to do their homework. Moreover, children who shared with their parent an understanding of their preferences for learning at home, had a more positive attitude toward homework than those who did not.

Unfortunately, unlike the findings reported by Hong and Lee (1999a), a shared understanding about preferences between child and parent was not related to homework achievement in the Perkins and Milgram (1996) study. The finding may represent a cultural difference between the three cultures, that is, the United States, Korea, and Hong Kong. Another possible explanation for this finding might be that although parents were well aware of the preferences of their children as to how they wanted to do their homework, in the United States the awareness was not manifested in the real situation in which the child did the homework. The shared child–parent understanding of homework preferences was probably part of the overall understanding of these parents about their children's personality characteristics. Such understanding results in more positive parent–child interactions in many life situations, which in turn are likely to result in better attitudes in children. Understanding by parents of their children's homework preferences might result in a more positive attitude toward homework. On the other hand, it is one thing for a parent to understand the child's preferences and quite another to accommodate it and allow the child to do homework that way. For example, a parent might understand that the child prefers to do homework while sprawled on the floor, with music playing, but adamantly refuses to allow this to occur. Perhaps in Hong Kong, parents were both aware of their children's homework preferences and allowed them to do their assignments that way; or many Chinese students already do their homework in the way their parents prefer them to do. The cultural differences in homework preferences discussed in the next chapter may further assist the understanding of these relationships.

Parents' Acceptance and Willingness to Accommodate Children's Homework Performance Preferences

The preceding section discussed the degree of parental awareness of children's preferences for doing homework. It is promising that many parents are indeed aware of how their children want to do their homework. However, even if parents understand and are aware of their children's pattern of personal preferences for doing homework, they may not make the effort required to match the actual situation in which the child does homework to the child's preferred conditions. We now turn to the question of whether parents who understand their children's preferences encourage their children to do homework under conditions of their own choosing.

In the earlier section, we discussed the studies on the gap between students' preferred and actual ways of doing homework, indicating that just as many learners do not learn in school according to their individual preferences, many do not do their homework according to their preferences either. In the Ohayon (1999) study, children characterized by low levels of creative thinking reported differences between the preferred and actual situation in which they did their homework that focused on three, easily remediable dimensions. They complained that they were provided with less light than they preferred. Moreover, they were not able to move about as they liked and had to remain seated and always in the same place when doing homework. In examining these representative examples of the specific findings of the study, it is striking to conclude that some relatively simple accommodation on the part of parents would result in much greater match between the preferred and the actual conditions under which children do their homework.

Learners are not always permitted to learn at home under their preferred conditions. Parents frequently have strong views about learning conditions and these views may be in contrast to the conditions preferred by the learner. For instance, a child might prefer to study with peers and may actually do better with peer cooperation. The parent, however, might not allow this mode of studying because he or she may feel that studying should be done alone, whereas friends are for socialization. The child might prefer to do his or her homework with background music, but the parent might not allow studying that way because the parent believes music will prevent concentration. It is important for parents to realize that accommodating home environment to the homework performance preferences of children can be a factor in improving the academic achievement level of the homework assignments. Ohayon (1999) computed a score that reflected the discrepancy between the preferred and actual conditions under which the child did his or her homework and found a correlation of $-.29$ between this gap score and perceived achievement on homework. In other words, the greater the gap, indicating low parent awareness, the lower the achievement. This finding should provide incentive for parents to increase understanding of their child's homework performance preferences and to accommodate the actual conditions under which homework is done.

Increasing Parental Awareness of and Accommodation to Children's Homework Performance Preferences

It has been assumed that at-home learning takes place under chosen or preferred conditions to a much greater extent than learning at school. The rationale for this view is that at school teachers, and not pupils, determine the conditions, but at home the child has a much greater choice about when, where, and how to study. The findings presented here indicate that this assumption may not be tenable and may indeed be more a goal than a reality. School systems need to give serious attention both to increasing awareness of homework motivation and preferences in children and in parents and to providing them with the information and techniques required to accommodate homework assignments to these preferences as well as their motivation levels and sources.

The findings reported make it clear that there are two possible reasons for parents not accommodating the learning conditions to children's preferences. One reason is that parents are unaware of their children's preferences and the second is that they are aware but unwilling to adjust to what the learner wants. In order to decrease the gap, it is important to clarify which reason explains the gap. Teachers and counselors must employ different approaches to increase awareness from those that would be used to create willingness to accommodate to the learner's preferences.

In summary, although parents may be aware of their child's preferences, they do not necessarily accept and respect them and do not always provide a homework environment that matches their child's preferences. It is a challenge to school systems to convey to parents the importance of matching homework environment with children's preferences. Additionally, teachers and counselors can provide parents with guidance on how to identify homework motivation and preferences and can encourage them to allow their children to do their homework under conditions that more closely match their preferences.

Homework has been a source of dissatisfaction for children and parents for decades. A large popular literature exists criticizing the use of homework. We call this "cursing the darkness." It is very easy to discuss what is wrong. It is a much greater challenge "to light a candle," that is, to suggest ways in which to improve the situation that is viewed as problematic. The remaining chapters are devoted to an effort "to light a candle" and to suggest what can be done to meet the challenge of making homework a more productive and pleasant part of the educational process.

4

Cultural, Gender, and Age Differences in Homework Motivation and Preference

In a recent study Milgram, Dunn, and Price (1993) compared the learning styles of approximately 6,000 children in Grades 7 through 12 in the following nine countries: the United States, Israel, Brazil, Canada, Korea, Guatemala, Philippines, Egypt, and Greece. They found clear, cross-cultural, in-school learning style differences in adolescents among the cultures studied. Price and Milgram (1993) summarized and interpreted the intricate findings on the specific differences of preferences among these nine cultures. Based on the findings of Hong, Milgram, and Perkins (1995) and Perkins and Milgram (1996) on the relationship between in-school and out-of-school learning styles, it seemed reasonable to expect that there would be cross-cultural differences in homework preferences similar to those obtained for in-school learning style preferences. In this chapter, we first present the findings on cultural and gender differences in homework motivation and preference. Then we discuss research findings on developmental changes in homework motivation and preference.

CULTURAL AND GENDER DIFFERENCES IN HOMEWORK MOTIVATION AND PREFERENCE

We investigated the cultural influence on students' homework motivation and preference in 273 U.S., 219 Korean, and 244 Hong Kong seventh-grade students. The research participants were 379 males and 357 females. Cultural differences in preferred actual homework styles were investigated in all three countries.

We first examined whether culture had an impact on gender differences in homework motivation and preference in each culture. There was a country × gender interaction effect on overall homework preference scores. The effect size, although rather small, indicated gender differences in a few components of homework performance were influenced by the culture. When each preference component was examined, only two components (design and place) showed an interaction effect with a discernible statistical significance ($p < .0005$).

In the design component, U.S. students preferred informal design of furniture (2.42 on a 5-point scale) when doing homework and both Korean (3.35) and Chinese students (3.81) preferred formal design, with Chinese students preferring it to an even greater extent. However, Korean female students, compared to males, preferred more formal design, whereas in the United States, the male students tended to prefer formal design more than the females. Chinese male and female students did not differ significantly in their preference of formal versus informal design of the furniture in their homes used in their study areas. A similar pattern was found with the place component: On the average, U.S students preferred doing their homework in different places in the home rather than in the same place all the time (2.88) compared to Korean (3.41) and Chinese (3.58) students. However, Korean and Chinese female students, compared to their male counterparts, indicated a higher preference for a set place in which to study in the home. Among the U.S. research participants, male students, more than the females, tended to prefer a set place in which to do their homework. Keeping in mind these two components, which showed interaction effects between gender and country, we examine cultural and gender differences in homework motivation and preference in each culture.

Cultural Differences

Cultural differences were significant on the overall homework motivation and preference scores ($p < .0005$). When each component was examined, cultural differences were significantly different in 13 components (all $ps < .0005$).

Motivational

Three of the five components were different among the three countries. U.S. students reported the highest self-motivation level for doing their homework well (4.13). There was no significant difference between Korean (3.66) and Chinese (3.62) students. The same pattern was found with the parent-motivated and teacher-motivated components: U.S. students reported their preference of doing homework well in order to satisfy their parents and teachers (3.74 and 3.80, respectively) more than Korean (2.92 and 3.38, respectively) and Chinese (3.19 and 3.44, respectively) students. Thus, in general, U.S. students were highly motivated by all three sources of motivation including self-, parent-, and teacher-motivation, compared to the learners in the two Asian countries.

Both the high self-perceived achievement level reported by U.S. students (chapter 5) and the current finding that U.S. students perceive their own level of motivation as high may well reflect a cultural difference. Asian students might possess a high standard as to the meaning of high motivation, thus rating their motivation level lower than that of U.S. students, who use a different standard for what constitutes high self-motivation. The differences on the parent- and teacher-motivated components may also be indicators of a cultural difference. Asian students may consider it best to be self-motivated and thus think that they need to be motivated less by parents or teachers than do students in the United States, where it may be more acceptable to be parent- or teacher-motivated. Here again, the findings may have been the result of cultural differences in the standard for what constitutes a high level of motivation. These differences can only be clarified by interviews with individual students, which is a worthy direction for future investigations. Persistence and responsibility did not show significant differences among the three countries, with average scores ranging between 3.46 and 3.63.

Organizational

Two of the three components in this category were significantly different among the three countries. Although there was no difference between U.S. (3.49) and Korean (3.43) students on the scores of the order component, students from both countries had significantly higher scores than those from Hong Kong (3.02). This finding indicates that students from the United States and Korea prefer to organize their homework assignments according to a set order that changes little each day, whereas those from Hong Kong did not. U.S. students prefer to do their homework in different places within their homes (2.88), whereas those from Korea (3.41) and Hong Kong (3.58) prefer to do homework in the same place. Homework structure preferences were not different among the three countries. Students in all three countries indicated their preferences for structured homework instructions and assignments. This is an interesting finding because we are calling for considerable flexibility and individualization of homework assignments to individual learners. This finding reveals that, although homework should be adjusted to accommodate preferences, more students prefer structured than unstructured homework assignments, indicating that many students have needs for understanding exactly what to do.

Surroundings

Three of the four surroundings components were significantly different among the students from the three countries. On the average, more
U.S. students preferred to have some sort of sound present while doing
homework (3.38), compared to students from Korea (2.56) and Hong
Kong (2.61); no difference was found between Korean and Chinese students. The cultural differences were apparent between students from the
United States and Asia, with more students of Western culture preferring
background sound. The light component showed a similar pattern: Students from Korea (4.04) and Hong Kong (4.00) preferred to have more
light compared to their U.S. counterparts (3.68). The design component's
average scores were different among all three countries. Students from
Hong Kong (3.82) preferred the most formal design, followed by those
from Korea (3.45), and then from the United States (2.42). Although both
Chinese and Korean students preferred a formal design, U.S. students
on the average preferred an informal design. No cultural difference was
found in temperature. These findings are similar to those reported by
Wallace (1995) in a study of elementary school students from the Philippines who were of a similar cultural background. These students also
preferred a quiet environment with bright light and a formal design in
school learning. In general, the cultural differences on the preferences of
home surroundings were largely along the line of Eastern and Western
culture.

Perceptual-Physical

Among the perceptual components, auditory and visual showed significant differences by country, whereas tactile and kinesthetic did not.
The three countries were different from one another in the auditory preference scores, with U.S. students showing the highest average score
(3.84), followed by Chinese (3.27) and then Korean students (2.64). The
opposite direction was found with visual preferences (2.44 in the United
States, 3.06 in Hong Kong, and 3.42 in Korea). U.S. students preferred to
hear their homework instructions, whereas Korean students preferred
visual instructions with Chinese students falling between the two, close
to the choice of uncertainty in their preferences. This might indicate that
U.S. students have been used to hearing homework instructions or need
to hear more explanations of the homework requirement, whereas the
opposite may be true for Korean students. Clear preferences for tactile
and kinesthetic learning were not reported by students from any of the
three countries. This might be because homework requiring tactile or
kinesthetic sources has not been given to students often enough for them
to have formulated a preference.

Both physical components were significantly different among the countries. On average, U.S. students scored highest (3.35) in food intake, followed by Chinese (3.05) and then Korean (2.88) students. The mobility component showed the same pattern, with the U.S. students scoring the highest (2.84), followed by the two other countries (2.54 and 2.52 for Chinese and Korean students, respectively). Again, these two physical components show the cultural differences along the line of Western and Eastern culture, indicating that Asian culture may be more strict in the sense that Asian students do not desire or are not permitted or desired to eat or move around the room when doing homework, whereas more freedom is granted to U.S. students.

Interpersonal

Although students from all three countries preferred not to have authority figures present while doing homework, U.S. scored highest (2.51), but there was no difference between Chinese (2.17) and Korean (2.10) students. Similar responses were obtained for alone–peers with students from all three countries reporting no particular preference either to work alone or with peers (2.82 to 2.99).

Conclusions

There is some similarity in students' homework motivation and preference in these three cultures. However, there are a substantial number of homework performance components that were clearly distinguished among children from the three cultures. Many of these cross-cultural differences reflect the norms of acceptable behavior in each culture. In Hong Kong and Korea, students are expected to study in formal study furniture (desk and chair). Listening to music, eating, drinking, and moving about while learning are more acceptable in the United States than in the two Asian countries. The pattern of preferences of the Asian students, as previously reported, would probably be considered by educators in many parts of the world to contribute to doing homework successfully. However, careful interpretation is needed because homework preferences constitute only a small part of a vast array of factors that affect academic achievement.

The findings regarding cultural differences on homework motivation and preference between youngsters in Korea and the United States are very similar to those reported by Hong, Milgram, and Perkins (1995) for fifth and sixth graders in the same two cultures. The new findings demonstrate that the cultural differences found in the earlier study obtain not only to elementary school-age children but to the junior high age as well. Teacher awareness of cultural differences in homework preferences would be helpful in understanding individual student choice or preference of the way students engage in homework or class work and might encourage teachers to assign homework tasks that are harmonious with student preferences. This would be especially desirable for teachers in the United States, where students come from various ethnic backgrounds.

Although there were some cross-cultural differences in homework motivation and preference in the three countries, they represent only a few of the many countries in the world. The investigation of homework motivation and preferences in the United States, Korea, and Hong Kong is an initial attempt to investigate the topic, but many more studies are required.

Gender Differences

A statistically significant gender difference was indicated on the overall scores of the preferred homework components in students in all three countries ($p < .0005$). As just discussed, country $\times$ gender interaction effects were shown in the two components (design and place). Keeping that in mind, the gender differences of preferred style components for each country are discussed here. Only those components with a significance level less than .005 are reported.

In the United States, gender differences were indicated only in the design and place components. Female students (2.24) preferred more informal furniture design than did male students (2.61). Again, female students (2.72) preferred to change place more rather than using a set place in the home, compared to male students (3.06). Interestingly, in studies of in-school learning styles, males more than females preferred an informal seating arrangement and some mobility (Dunn, Ginnitti, et al., 1990; Yong & McIntyre, 1992). In school, most classroom chairs are made of hard materials. Male students, as compared to their female counterparts, have less padding in their buttocks which may cause male students to prefer informal seating where they can move their bodies more freely. In the home, that variable is no longer a determining factor because students can choose their seating arrangement. That is, preferences to formal or informal design may not be necessarily determined by biological need.

In Korea, five components showed gender differences. Korean female students (3.63) preferred formal design more than did male students (3.09), and females (3.97) also preferred more structured homework instructions than did male students (3.65). Male students (3.11) were more parent-motivated, compared to females (2.70). Males preferred homework that required tactile (3.23) and kinesthetic (3.38) work, compared to females (2.95 and 2.59, respectively). In Hong Kong, the multivariate analysis result did not reach a significant level, with one univariate significance found in the kinesthetic component. More male Chinese students (3.34) preferred homework that involved kinesthetic work than did females (3.05).

In summary, in all three countries, more similarities than differences were indicated between gender. Korean students showed more gender differences than did U.S. or Chinese students, with females preferring more structured homework and formal design, and males preferring work that involves tactile or kinesthetic activity. The difference in the number of significant findings between Korean and Chinese and U.S. students is interesting. It is difficult to conjecture as to why gender differences were not found in Chinese students in Hong Kong. Hong Kong had been a British-governed territory that became a Special Administrative Region of the People's Republic of China in 1997. One could speculate that the finding reflects a view of gender equity that characterizes the Hong Kong educational system more than the Korean system because of the strong British influence on education in one and not the other culture. A similar speculation could be applied to the U.S. system, where gender equity in classrooms has been and is being sought. However, this speculation is quite a leap from the current findings. More replication studies are needed to clarify these differences.

AGE DIFFERENCES IN PREFERRED AND ACTUAL HOMEWORK PERFORMANCE

We examined whether a consistent developmental pattern exists in students' preferred and actual ways of doing homework. Again, the same subjects from two of the countries, the United States and Korea, were examined. In both countries, the age difference was significant ($ps < .005$) on overall preferred or actual measures. A follow-up univariate examination on each homework motivation and preference component was conducted. We present only those with a significance level less than .005.

In the United States, more seventh graders (3.69) than fifth graders (3.40) preferred to do their homework in bright light. Persistence level declined from fifth (3.88) to seventh grade (3.63), and seventh graders (3.76) reported being less motivated by parents than did fifth graders (4.05). Both tactile and kinesthetic preference levels declined from fifth (3.57 and 3.54, respectively) to seventh grade (3.21 and 3.23, respectively). A tendency toward a preference to study with peers was reported more by seventh graders (3.00), compared to fifth graders (2.69); however, they preferred not to have an adult figure present more strongly (2.54) than did fifth graders (2.98). Other components did not reveal developmental changes.

Thus, compared to younger students, older U.S. students preferred to do their homework in a well-lighted area, with peers, but without a supervising adult figure. The developmental change from preferring to study alone to studying with peers and from preferring more to less adult supervision when doing homework can be seen as a predictable and expected course of sociological development. That is, as children mature, they tend to dislike parental involvement in their affairs, whereas the opposite trend occurs with reference to association with their friends. The decrease with age in the parent-motivated score may also indicate this tendency.

The increasing difficulty or kinds of homework content may be one of the reasons for the decline in the persistence, tactile, and kinesthetic levels. As homework becomes more difficult and lengthy in the upper grades, students might lose their persistence for completing homework if they view the assignments as difficult to complete. Teachers need to take into account students' competence levels when designing homework assignments in order to reduce frustration by homework failure and to increase patience, persistence, and success in homework completion. As compared to elementary school-level homework, homework assignments given to junior high school students are probably less hands-on and experiential, and hence require less tactile or kinesthetic work. Although the underlying reasons for this change is not clear, the data may suggest that schools should provide a variety of homework assignments involving a variety of perceptual modalities.

Only three motivational components showed significant changes. Levels of self-motivation, parent-motivation, and persistence for homework declined in older students. The tendency for changes in a negative direction in older students is certainly disturbing and requires the attention of both teachers and parents.

In Korea, more older students preferred structured homework (3.81) and to have a set place in which to do their homework (3.41) than did younger students (3.55 and 3.15, respectively). As found in the U.S. sample, both parent-motivated and teacher-motivated scores declined in seventh grade (2.92 and 3.38, respectively) as compared to fifth grade (3.56 and 3.73, respectively). Unlike U.S. students, Korean seventh graders (2.82) more than fifth graders (3.11) preferred to do their homework alone. Whereas fifth graders (3.37) preferred a warmer environment in which to do homework, seventh graders (2.97) did not reveal a strong preference for a particular room temperature. The reason for a decline in preference for a warm learning environment cannot be interpreted due to a lack of studies in this area.

Findings with actual homework performance were similar to those of preferences, but with fewer components showing developmental changes in both countries. Older Korean students actually did their homework in a cooler environment (2.92) and by themselves rather than with peers (2.48), and were less parent-motivated (2.78), compared to younger students (3.32, 2.72, and 2.78, respectively). However, the structure, place, and teacher-motivated components did not show a pattern of developmental change that corresponded to those that were obtained in the preferred measure. One additional component that indicated change with age was responsibility, in which seventh graders (3.30) reported a lower level than did fifth graders (3.51). The same pattern occurred in U.S. students in self- and parent-motivated and responsibility components.

In summary, developmental changes were evident in both countries. Some of these changes seem quite understandable in terms of what is known about the process of personal–social development—older students show independence, prefer no adult supervision, and are less concerned about satisfying their parents by doing homework. In both countries, there were fewer developmental changes in scores of actual rather than those of preferred homework performance. Consistent findings in both countries indicate that students' preferred way of studying might neither have been respected nor actually applied over the years, thus only showing changed in a small number of actual component measures. However, students perceived some of their preferred ways of studying differently as they grew older, whether or not the preferences were regarded.

An interesting cultural difference was found with the alone–peers component: Although older U.S. students preferred to work with friends more than their younger counterparts, Korean students demonstrated an opposite trend, that is, older more than younger students preferred to work alone. Studying with friends or engaging in other social activities after school rarely occurs in Korea due to long school hours and extra learning activities after school. Thus, not having the time available to do homework with peers might have led these students to become accustomed to doing homework alone.

In a study with Chinese-Canadian children, Leung (1993) found that older children felt homework to be less important and useful, liked school and homework less, and showed a weaker sense of responsibility for homework than did younger children. Additionally, as compared to younger children, older students perceived their parents to value schoolwork less, were less concerned about their schoolwork, and showed less positive feelings about good school performance. These developmental changes in a negative direction in children's own views toward school and in their perceptions of their parents' views toward school and homework, are indicators of where teachers, principals, and school counselors might well focus their attention. Serious efforts should be made to improve children's attitudes toward school. It would be helpful to arrange for learning at school and at home to match students' learning preferences. Both teachers and parents must understand students' homework motivation and preferences. Teachers can help by accommodating homework assignments to student preferences, and parents can help by providing a favorable homework environment for their children.

It is well-documented that when students are taught through their learning preferences, they learn better in school and attain more enjoyment from the learning process (Dunn & Dunn, 1992, 1993; S. Sims & Sims, 1995). The information on cultural, gender, and age differences in homework motivation and preferences provided here can serve a practical purpose. Combined with information on the individual child's homework motivation and preference profile, these findings would help parents and teachers acquire a broader knowledge base on the topic and encourage them to attempt customization of homework assignments and homework conditions to the needs of the individual learners. This is likely to increase student achievement and to improve their attitudes toward homework. The remaining chapters suggest a number of intervention strategies that explain more specifically how parents, teachers, and students can cooperate as a team in this endeavor.

5

Relationship of Homework Motivation and Preference to Achievement and Attitude toward Homework

Many educators believe that homework contributes to the improvement of school learning and academic achievement (Cooper, 1989a; Walberg, Paschal, & Weinstein, 1985). Accordingly, homework is a frequently used teaching strategy in schools throughout the world. A number of popular magazines such as *Parents Magazine* and *Times-Educational Supplement* often deal with the homework issue; books and articles offering advice on helping children with homework have been published (e.g., Bursuck, 1995; Rosemond, 1990; Wood, 1987); homework policy guidelines have been produced for school administrators (e.g., Cooper, 1994); and educational intervention programs have been developed to ensure the productive accomplishment of homework (e.g., Anesko, Schoiock, Ramirez, & Levine, 1987; Epstein, 1998; Rosenberg, 1995).

Despite the considerable interest on the part of parents and educators about homework, both theoretical and empirical articles on the subject reflect contradictory views on homework's effectiveness (see chapter 1 for detail). These inconsistent views may be due to the inadequate theoretical and operational definition of the homework factors affecting students' academic achievement and attitude. Although studies of homework effects on achievement have focused on the characteristics of the homework itself (e.g., type, quality, amount, and feedback approach), individual differences of the students doing the homework received relatively little attention. This book, in general, focuses on learners, and this chapter, in particular, examines the very important question of how the homework preferences of an individual affect his or her homework achievement and attitude.

There have been a considerable number of studies on individual, cultural, and gender differences in in-school learning styles or preferences, and the effects on achievement of matching learning environment to learner preferences (e.g., Callan, 1996; Dunn, Beaudry, & Klavas, 1989; Dunn & Griggs, 1990; Dunn, Griggs, & Price, 1993; Hodgin & Wooliscroft, 1997; Milgram et al., 1993; Renzulli & Reis, 1998). These studies were conducted in school classrooms, and in-school learning style inventories (e.g., Dunn et al., 1987) were used to identify student learning styles. We assert that just as every student has a characteristic school learning style, each also has a characteristic style for learning outside of school. Studies on out-of-school learning style have indicated that learning style in school and out of school are related, yet are empirically distinguishable (Hong, Milgram, & Perkins, 1995; Perkins & Milgram, 1996). We examined the relationship of homework motivation and preference to student achievement using an instrument, described in chapter 2, specifically designed to assess home learning. The findings are summarized here.

HOMEWORK MOTIVATION AND PREFERENCE AND STUDENT ACHIEVEMENT

Whether having particular homework preferences would affect homework and academic achievement and attitude toward homework was examined. Due to a large number of factors influencing student achievement and because the research was not a controlled experimental study, large effects were not expected. However, we expected that there would be some consistent patterns in some of the homework motivation and preference components that distinguish students who achieve at a high academic level and who have a positive attitude toward their homework from those who are not high achieving or who have less positive attitudes toward homework.

Data were collected on homework motivation and preference, homework and academic achievement, and students' own perception of their homework achievement and attitude from seventh-grade students in the United States (134 males and 138 females) and fifth- and seventh-grade Chinese students (172 males and 157 females and 130 males and 114 females, respectively) (Hong, 1998; Hong & Lee, 1999a). Additionally, in this chapter we include discussion of findings from other studies that are relevant because they add to the understanding of the question under investigation. As indicated earlier, the reports provided here are not based on intervention studies, but from the self-report of students' homework motivation and preference, homework achievement and attitude, and teacher-rated homework and academic achievement.

Patterns of Homework Motivation and Preference in Different Levels of Achievement and Attitude

Distinctive learning preferences were observed in low- and high-achieving students in some of the motivation and preference components. However, the two different measures of achievement (self-perceived vs. teacher-rated achievement scores) revealed large differences in the number of motivation and preference components that distinguished the two achievement groups. More distinguishing components were found with the self-perceived homework achievement and attitude levels than with the teacher-rated achievement levels. For example, in the U.S. seventh graders, whereas 5 or less style elements distinguished the three levels of teacher-rated homework and academic achievement, 10 or more components distinguished the self-perceived homework achievement levels. These findings were consistent over the two studies that examined children of the same age (seventh graders) (Hong, 1998; Hong & Lee, 1999a).

The findings may indicate that students' self-perceived homework achievement and attitude reflect their homework behavior (the way they prefer to do their homework) more closely than do teacher-rated achievement measures. Teacher-rated achievement may be explained by many factors other than the pattern of homework preferences that were investigated in this study (e.g., aptitude, previous achievement level). Although short-term effects of homework efforts and attitudes on school achievement may not be readily evident, if students' homework preferences are actually accommodated by teachers and parents, it is reasonable to expect that students' homework and school achievement will be increased, as was evidenced in in-school learning style studies.

Group Differences on Homework Motivation and Preference

Motivational

Different patterns of homework style were found in high and low homework achievers and between those children with positive and negative attitudes toward homework. It was not surprising to find that the motivational components distinguished the levels of all types of achievement and attitude toward homework. That is, students in the high-achieving group were more self-motivated, persistent, prompt, and responsible in doing their homework than were those in the low-achieving group.

A study comparing students with learning disabilities (LD) to nondisabled students to determine if certain practices might be related to failure to complete homework assignments also showed a similar pattern (Gajria & Salend, 1995). Students with LD reported low levels of motivation compared to their nondisabled age peers. For example, they were less persistent (reflected by higher ratings on items such as "lose interest in homework after working for 30 minutes on homework," "quit doing homework if it appears difficult") and less responsible ("must be reminded to start homework," "takes a long time to start homework"). Students with LD also had a less favorable attitude toward homework ("complains about homework") (Gajria & Salend, 1995; Polloway, Epstein, & Foley, 1992).

Students' self-perception of their work at home was positive in those who reported themselves to be highly motivated by parents. Similarly a high level of teacher-rated achievement (both homework completion and quality and final examination scores) was associated with those students who were teacher-motivated (with one exception in Chinese seventh graders where parent-motivated students scored high in homework completion). Among U.S. students, those in the high homework achievement group (both self-perceived and teacher-rated) were more parent- and teacher-motivated than were their low-achieving age peers, whereas high academic achievers were more teacher-motivated, but not more parent-motivated, than were their low-achieving age peers.

Taken together, the findings from these studies suggest that parents have a more significant role in the home study environment, whereas teachers are more influential in school learning. However, both parents and teachers are influential in motivating students both directly and indirectly. This trend is seen in the findings of the studies that used teacher-rated homework scores in which both parents and teachers seem to influence the motivation of work at home.

Organizational

Organizational preferences (structure, order, place) were differentiated only by the self-perceived homework achievement and attitude measures, with high-achieving and high positive attitude students preferring to work on the structured homework, to organize the work in some order, and to use the same spot in the house. However, differences in these components did not make differences in the teacher-rated achievement scores. Students with LD when compared to their nondisabled counterparts were also less organized ("is unsure about which homework to start first") (Gajria & Salend, 1995).

Surroundings

Students who perceived their homework achievement level as being high preferred a quiet and well-lit environment and formal study furniture (desk and chair) when doing their homework. Reasonably, students with positive attitudes toward homework also preferred a quiet and formal design, but did not have specific preferences toward lighting or temperature. Although there were some significant findings on lighting and design with teacher-rated achievement levels, the effects were too small to interpret the findings meaningfully.

Perceptual-Physical

No perceptual modality (auditory, visual, tactile, kinesthetic) distinguished the high- and low-achieving students of all achievement types, except for the two small effects found in Chinese fifth graders (tactile with self-perceived homework achievement and visual with homework quality). The strong perceptual modalities are indeed individual preferences of the way they study, and no specific perceptual strength promotes the achievement and attitude. That is, individual differences are great within each achievement group as well as between groups. It is then important to pay particular attention to the individual perceptual strengths regardless of from which achievement group particular individual students came. However, the physical sensitivity scores, more strongly the intake than the mobility component, were differentiated by the high–low levels of some achievement and attitude scores. That is, low-achieving students preferred to eat or drink and to move about when they do their homework, compared to their high-achieving peers.

Interpersonal

The group differences of students' preferences in the alone–peers and authority figure present components were not consistent over the grade levels or the achievement types. In many instances, the differences were not significant. However, when the statistical significance was found, consistent patterns emerged: High-achieving students preferred to do homework alone or to have an adult figure present when they do homework.

Group Differences and Subject Matters:
Preferred–Actual Gap

There were three actual but not preferred components found to differentiate the groups. Although they did not "prefer" to do so, more students who perceived a low homework achievement reported that they actually changed places rather than did homework in the same place, ate and drank, and moved about the room when they did their homework than those who perceived their achievement high. An interesting finding in both mathematics and English achievement was that although high achievers reported that they were teacher-motivated in actual situations, they were not different from low achievers in their preference measure of motivation.

When the distinguishing components were compared for academic achievement levels in two different subject matters, more similarities than differences were indicated. The differences found are worth noting. For example, in U.S. seventh graders, mathematics achievement levels were differentiated by five actual homework performance components (self-motivated, teacher-motivated, persistence, structure, and alone–peers), whereas English achievement levels were differentiated by three elements (self-motivated, teacher-motivated, and light). These findings may indicate that homework motivation and preferences are more characteristically different in high–low mathematics achievers than in high–low English achievers. However, when their preferred (instead of actual) measures were analyzed, distinguishing components were the same in both subject matter (self-motivated, light, and intake).

Summary

Although there are some components that did not distinguish students in different levels of achievement, many did. The differences have been shown in low-versus high-achieving school-aged students as well as in college-level students, and LD versus nondisabled students (e.g., Gajria & Salend, 1995; Onwuegbuzie & Daley, 1997; Sparks, 1990). In general, no matter which types of achievement groups the components of homework motivation and preference differentiated, the direction and patterns of distinguishing components were the same across the studies with students from different countries. For example, students in high achievers were more self-, parent-, and teacher-motivated; persistent; organized their homework in a certain order; preferred or did homework in a bright home environment; did homework by themselves rather than with peers; preferred structured homework than were their low-achieving counterparts.

Most of the distinguishing components described here were found in students from both countries, but there were a few that were specific to a certain country. This might indicate cultural influence on homework motivation and preferences (see chapter 3 for cultural differences). However, the consistency of the findings across the different countries is remarkable, suggesting there are common components that affect achievement and attitudes of school children, thus indicating the importance of understanding and using children's homework motivation and preferences in homework studies and interventions. Although group differences have been found in achievement levels, gender, age, and culture, it is critical to keep in mind that individual differences in homework motivation and preferences are the principal information that should be used in efforts to accommodate student preferences. However, the knowledge of these group differences would be useful when teachers and parents wish to augment student learning preferences by supplementing their primary preferences (see chapter 9).

RELATIONSHIP OF HOMEWORK AMOUNT TO HOMEWORK ACHIEVEMENT AND ATTITUDE

As students advance from elementary to high school, the amount of homework increases and, accordingly, so does the amount of time needed to complete assignments. Studies investigating the time students spend on homework indicate a steady increase from low to high grade levels (Polloway, Epstein, Bursuck, Jayanthi, & Cumblad, 1995; Roderique, Polloway, Cumblad, Epstein, & Bursuch, 1995).

Although the amount of time spent on homework was correlated with student achievement in most surveys, especially in high school students (Cooper & Nye, 1994), student attitude toward homework decreased as the amount of homework increased (Cooper et al., 1998). With students' reported time spent for homework showing a negative relationship with homework attitude, it is reasonable to expect that students' self-perceived homework amount (instead of time spent) would also show a negative relationship with their attitudes toward homework. If homework amount is excessive in the students' views, it is likely that their attitudes toward it would be negative.

However, unlike the positive relationship shown between homework achievement and homework amount as measured by time spent completing homework, the relationship of homework achievement and homework amount perceived by students has not been studied. Based on previous studies, we speculate that the latter relationship would be negative, if not significant, whereas the relationship between perceived homework achievement and homework attitude would be positive. We examined these relationships using the data from 97 Grade 7 and 62 Grades 9 and 10 students in the United States, and 244 Grade 5 and 329 Grade 7 Chinese students in Hong Kong.

The relationship among self-perceived homework amount, homework achievement, and homework attitude showed the expected direction in both age groups. As expected, students' perceived homework amount was negatively related with homework attitude ($-.34$ and $-.44$ in the U.S. middle and high school students, respectively, and $-.52$ and $-.56$

in Chinese fifth and seventh graders, respectively). That is, students who thought that the amount of homework is excessive tended to have negative attitude.

Students who view the homework amount as excessive also perceived their homework achievement to be low ($-.18$ and $-.25$, statistically nonsignificant, in the U.S. middle and high school students, respectively, and $-.21$ and $-.29$ in Chinese fifth and seventh graders, respectively). The reasons for perceiving the homework amount as they did were not examined and thus the underlying reasons for its relationship with attitude and achievement could not be explained properly. However, we do know that the amount and attitude are closely and negatively related, and the negative attitude toward homework would in turn influence negatively on the homework achievement. The relationship between the perceived homework attitude and achievement were .33 and .35 in U.S. middle and high school students, respectively, and .45 and .57 in Chinese fifth and seventh graders, respectively.

Another interesting finding was the level of self-perceived homework achievement in various countries. In three of the four items measuring perceived homework achievement, U.S. seventh-grade students, when compared with Korean or Chinese same-age peers, reported having a higher level of homework achievement (Hong & Milgram, 1999). For example, when the items involve judging their own homework achievement (e.g., doing a good job on homework, doing homework correctly, getting a high grade if grades were given), the average of U.S. students' scores was significantly higher (3.79 out of 5) than that of Korean and Chinese students' (3.25 and 3.39, respectively). In general, U.S. students perceived their homework achievement higher than students from Asia. Although it is conceivable that U.S. students' perception of their homework achievement reflect their actual level of achievement, it is also possible that the standard for what constitutes the high level of achievement between these countries might be different. Another cultural difference that could also be a possible explanation for this finding is that Asian students might be less demonstrative than U.S. students in expressing their own achievement level.

Relationship patterns among homework amount and homework attitude and achievement were similar in all samples, as described previously. Findings on students' homework perception in these studies add to the understanding of the importance of these perceptions in homework intention considerations. How students perceive homework assignments affects homework behavior. Using the information on the perceived homework amount, teachers can individualize the homework amount as part of their intervention approaches.

MATCH VERSUS MISMATCH BETWEEN PREFERRED AND ACTUAL HOMEWORK PERFORMANCE AND ITS RELATIONSHIP WITH HOMEWORK ACHIEVEMENT

In chapter 3, we analyzed the similarities and differences between students' preferred and actual ways of doing homework. Although there are similarities between them (i.e., some students actually do use their preferred ways and modes when doing homework), the score differences found between the two constructs indicate that some students' preferences were not applied in their actual homework situations. In this section, we analyze the degree of match between the preferred and actual measures for each component and examine whether there would be any significant differences in the homework achievement between students in the match versus mismatch group in U.S. seventh graders.

Note again that the analysis is based on self-reported data, that is, no intervention to actually match students' preferred with actual homework environment was attempted in this study. Thus, the match–mismatch group effects on homework components are expected to be smaller than what would have resulted if an intervention was implemented.

Degree of Match between Students' Preferred and Actual Homework Performance

The difference scores between preferred and actual measures of homework performance were computed for each component for each participant. The no-difference score in a component means that the preferred and actual scores were the same. The larger the difference score, the larger the difference between the preferred and actual scores.

The frequencies of each component's difference scores ranged from 0 (no difference between preferred and actual scores) to 4 (the largest difference between the two scores). A difference score of 4 indicates that a student's responses to preferred and actual measures on an item were 1 (*strongly disagree*) and 5 (*strongly agree*) or vice versa. Mean scores and frequencies in percentages for no difference, equal to or greater than 1, and those in between are presented in Table 5.1.

As indicated in the table, the mean difference scores ranged from .51 to .76, thus indicating that the average difference between the preferred and actual scores was less than 1. The percentages of no-difference ranged from 8 to 28, whereas those of the preferred–actual differences that were equal to or greater than 1 ranged from 15 to 33. As was discussed in chapter 3 on the preferred–actual gap, this finding also indicates that although there are students who actually do their homework

Table 5.1
Means and Standard Deviations and Frequencies in Percentages of the
Difference Scores between Preferred and Actual Measures

Homework style element	Mean (SD)	Difference score (%)		
		= 0	>0 and <1	≥ 1
Motivational source				
Self-motivated	.51 (.46)	20%	62%	18%
Parent-motivated	.55 (.51)	17	61	22
Teacher-motivated	.57 (.52)	21	54	25
Motivational strength				
Persistence	.54 (.51)	17	68	15
Responsibility	.71 (.65)	13	56	31
Organizational				
Structure	.73 (.58)	23	49	28
Set order	.65 (.52)	19	50	31
Set place	.62 (.49)	14	62	24
Environmental				
Sound	.53 (.54)	22	58	20
Light	.51 (.47)	21	58	21
Temperature	.62 (.64)	22	52	26
Design	.56 (.51)	16	62	22
Perceptual-Physical				
Auditory	.73 (.76)	26	41	33
Visual	.72 (.76)	28	39	33
Tactile	.67 (.55)	15	56	29
Kinesthetic	.61 (.58)	21	52	27
Intake	.65 (.61)	18	53	29
Mobility	.67 (.55)	8	63	29
Interpersonal				
Alone/peers	.76 (.68)	13	54	33
Authority figures	.68 (.56)	15	54	31

in their preferred home environments and modes, there are quite a few students who do not.

Differences in Student Achievement in Matched versus Mismatched Group

We compared achievement scores for students in the matched and mismatched groups. Students with difference scores between the preferred and actual measures less than 0.5 were assigned to the matched group, and those with the difference scores equal to or greater than 1 were assigned to the mismatched group. Students falling between the two criteria were excluded from this analysis. Only univariate tests with statistically significant results are reported here. The examined dependent measures were the four items of self-perceived homework achievement and mathematics and English final examination scores.

As expected, significant group differences on achievement were indicated mostly in the motivational components. Students who liked to do well on homework and actually reported that they did their best on homework (self-motivated) perceived their achievement level higher (4.02, matched group) than did those whose preferred and actual self-motivation levels were not matched (3.39, mismatched group). Students whose preferred and actual persistence level were matched did well on the mathematics exam (81.94), compared to those in the mismatched group (75.62).

Students who both preferred to do and actually do their homework in such a way that their parents would be satisfied (matched group) had high scores on perceived homework achievement (3.91), compared to students in the mismatched group (3.61). The match between preferred and actual measures in teacher-motivated component distinguished the high- and low-level achievement in both self-perceived homework and academic achievement. Students who liked to and actually did please their teacher by doing their homework well (matched group) showed higher self-perceived homework scores (3.93), compared to their mismatched peers (3.57). Additionally, students in the matched group scored higher in mathematics (82.50) and English (80.33) examinations than did their peers in the mismatched group (75.52 and 73.92, respectively).

Other components that showed matched versus mismatched group differences were design, place, auditory, kinesthetic. Students whose preference to a certain design of furniture matched with actual use of that furniture scored higher on an item of the perceived homework achievement than did their peers in the mismatched group: 3.98 versus 3.45 for "When doing my homework, I do a good job."

When students who preferred to get homework instructions from teachers through an auditory channel actually received them that way, they had a higher perception of homework achievement on all four items (3.90, average) than did their peers in the mismatched group (3.67). Students who preferred to do and actually did do their homework with the level of kinesthetic sense of their choice (experiments or actual experience) reported a higher level perception in two items of the homework achievement measure than did their peers in the mismatched group: 3.78 versus 3.42 for "If grades were given for homework, I would get a high grade"; and 3.99 versus 3.61 for "When doing my homework, I do a good job."

An interesting finding occurred with the place component. Those students whose preference on the place component (doing their homework in the same place or in a variety of places) did not match with the actual place (mismatched group) showed higher scores in the two homework achievement items than did their peers in the matched group: 3.91 versus 3.52 for "If grades were given for homework, I would get a high grade"; and 4.11 versus 3.73 for "I do my homework correctly." Inspection of the preferred and actual scores in the mismatched group indicated that there were more students whose actual score was higher than the preferred score, where the high score indicated the use of the same place. Thus, the finding may indicate that scores of students who actually use the same place when doing homework, even if they prefer to change places, are related to high perceived homework achievement. This is consistent with the finding that high-achieving students in general actually do their homework in the same place. This finding also points to the need for continuous monitoring by parents when they apply the HMPP information in the homework intervention and for supplementing students' preferences with other approaches in efforts to increase homework achievement.

Our knowledge of the group differences in homework motivation and achievement and of the effect of preferred–actual match versus mismatch and of parent–child match versus mismatch (i.e., parental awareness in chapter 3) on the homework achievement and attitude should be helpful when educators and parents plan homework interventions, especially when strategies for supplementing students' preferences are needed (see chapter 9).

6

Homework Motivation and Preference of Gifted and Talented Learners

Because their abilities differ from the norm, gifted students do not derive full benefit from the regular school program. If gifted students are to realize their potential, there must be adjustments both in the in-school and in the out-of-school learning program. If this is not done, their abilities and talents may be lost. The irony is that it probably is easier for teachers to offer special, challenging homework assignments for these students than it is to modify the curriculum that is offered in the classroom. In order to discuss appropriate learning situations for gifted students, in and out of school, it is necessary first to define what is meant by *gifted*.

This chapter is divided into four sections. The first section focuses on the danger of talent loss in gifted and talented learners. The second section defines *giftedness* and the need for a multidimensional formulation of the phenomenon. The third section reports research findings on the in-school and out-of-school learning styles of gifted students. The final section offers some implications of the views and research findings presented in the chapter.

TALENT LOSS

Talent loss is one of society's major problems because it is the waste of a precious natural resource. *Talent loss* is the failure of an adult to realize the potential abilities that he or she demonstrated as a youth. To realize ability means to actualize it by generating real-world products. It is not only a personal tragedy when adults fail to fulfill the promise of their youth, but the world also loses abilities that might have produced extraordinary contributions in all realms of human endeavor. One reason for talent loss is that the abilities of some gifted and talented young people are not identified in their homes and schools and efforts are not made to develop and enhance them.

The list of successful and productive gifted adults whose talents were almost lost is legendary. The eminent scientist, Albert Einstein, according to an apocryphal story, failed mathematics in elementary school. Steve Wozniak, developer of the first Apple home computer, was a high school dropout. Bill Gates, president of Microsoft, the largest producer of computer software in the world, dropped out of Harvard. There is a danger in these happy-ending stories. They serve to confirm the popular prejudice that most or all gifted children will realize their talents without educational intervention. Such, however, is not the situation. Many gifted youngsters fail to realize their potential abilities. There is little doubt that the list of individuals who are not famous because their talents were actually lost is very long indeed.

One important reason for failure to recognize in children and youth the abilities that later emerge as remarkable life achievements in adults is the difference between *remarkable accomplishments* in children and in adults. In children, general intellectual ability continues to be the major and, in many instances, the decisive criterion for defining giftedness. High IQ scores and high scholastic achievement in children are assumed to be indicators of remarkable attainments to come. Giftedness in adults, however, is quite different because it is not a test score but rather actual extraordinary achievement in a specific domain. In adults, giftedness is manifested in focused interest, ability, and activity. Adults are not gifted in general; they are gifted in something—music, mathematics, or languages, for example. In gifted adults, the realization of potential ability is reflected in a real-world product such as a musical score or a scientific breakthrough. Accordingly, with rare exception, children are not actually, and are at best potentially, gifted. Children are not expected to generate extraordinary products that meet the stringent standards of the real world. Children whose abilities are unconventional, that is, different from the abilities customarily accepted as indicators of giftedness (e.g., school grades, standardized IQ and achievement tests) are especially good candidates for talent loss. They are frequently not identified as gifted and are not given opportunities for special enrichment and acceleration that would have helped develop their potential talent.

The difference between the definition of giftedness in children and in adults cited here is probably the most basic overall explanation for talent loss. One reason for the difference in definition of giftedness in children and adults is the narrow view of giftedness in children that dominated the field for many years (Terman, 1925; Terman & Oden, 1947, 1959). Although there have been some promising developments in recent years (Gagné, 1995; Gardner, 1983; Renzulli, 1986; Sternberg & Davidson, 1986; Tannenbaum, 1983), it takes a long time for new concepts such as these to impact the real world of education (Cassidy & Hossler, 1992). One of the reasons for the gap between developing a theoretical understanding of giftedness and the IQ-oriented definition of giftedness routinely used in school systems is the lack of reliable and valid psychometric measures that are required in order to provide a practical means of identifying the vast array of component abilities postulated in the newer formulations.

THE CONCEPTUALIZATION AND ASSESSMENT OF GIFTEDNESS

Some types of giftedness are familiar to most people, and when they hear the word *gifted* they think of intellectual geniuses with extraordinarily high IQs or perhaps of artists or musicians with exceptional talent. There are kinds of giftedness that are less familiar but no less important. For example, Boris Yeltsin, the former president of Russia, was expelled from high school for showing leadership in adolescence. He stood up at a school assembly and incited his fellow high school students to rebel against the tyrannical principal. Laura Pederson made headlines when she retired from her business on Wall Street as a millionaire at age 22. Her classmates were surprised at her choice of career because they remembered that she never received very good grades in mathematics. Pederson once explained this seeming contradiction by saying, "Once they put dollar signs in front of the numbers, I understood everything perfectly!"

What do these two people who seem so different have in common? They are gifted, gifted in different ways, but gifted. *Giftedness* may be defined as extraordinary, that is, unusual and high-quality achievement in a specific domain. The accomplishments of both Yeltsin and Pederson meet this stringent criterion, Yeltsin in social leadership and Pederson in the business world. In this chapter we explain that the concept of giftedness, as it is correctly understood, can include not only high IQ-type genius and virtuoso aesthetic talent but also people, like Yeltsin and Pederson, who have extraordinary abilities in a wide variety of socially valuable domains.

In the 1980s a new era was ushered in when expanded, multifaceted views of giftedness symbolized by the widespread adoption of the terminology *gifted and talented* were introduced. Several edited volumes appeared summarizing the better-known multidimensional conceptualizations of giftedness (Cohen & Ambrose, 1993; Horowitz & O'Brien,

1985; Runco & Albert, 1990; Sternberg & Davidson, 1986). As part of this accelerated theoretical development, Milgram (1989, 1991) and Hong (in preparation) postulated comprehensive and integrative multidimensional models that explain giftedness as the result of the complex interaction of cognitive, personal–social, and sociocultural influences.

It has been suggested that domain-specific creative talent is a more valid predictor of significant life accomplishment later in life than conventional IQ scores and school grades (Hong, Milgram, & Whiston, 1993; Milgram & Hong, 1994; Milgram, Hong, Shavit, & Peled, 1997; Wallach & Wing, 1969; Wing & Wallach, 1971). Domain-specific creative talent is operationally defined in adults by their unusual and high-quality products in a specific domain (e.g., a scientific discovery, a mathematical formula, a symphony, a dramatic production). These kinds of products are rare in children and adolescents. Extraordinary attainments are unlikely to develop in many domains until people are older and have acquired the requisite life experience. However, there is often a passion and a commitment to a specific domain at a young age.

Accordingly, Milgram (1989, 1991) suggested that one way to identify specific creative talent in children and adolescents before these abilities become fully realized—that is, before there is an actual product in one's vocation—is to examine the quantity and quality of out-of-school activities and accomplishments. She asserted that domain-specific creative, intrinsically motivated, out-of-school activities done by young people for their own enjoyment and by their own choice, and not in order to fulfill school requirements or to earn grades or credits, may be precursors of talented adult accomplishments. The Tel-Aviv Activities and Accomplishments Inventory (TAAI) was developed to measure out-of-school activities and creative accomplishments in 11 specific domains (Milgram, 1973, 1983, 1987, 1990; 1998). The TAAI is unique in that specific psychometric measures are recommended to operationally define each of its postulated components. Educators and researchers are not only advised about how important it is to change procedures for identification of the gifted, but are provided with new procedures in the form of specific, easily available, and highly usable tools.

The multidimensional view of giftedness presented in many modern theories makes it clear that schools must strive to customize the teaching–learning process for gifted and talented children. The best place to individualize instruction and to differentiate curriculum from an early age is in the regular classroom. This may seem to some to be an impossible mission, an impossible dream. However, in a volume edited by Milgram (1989), authorities in a wide variety of subject matter areas presented detailed descriptions of approaches and techniques that provide classroom teachers with the tools required to customize specific school subjects for gifted learners. These chapters were intended to serve as an example of what can be done. Since 1989, vast technological advances associated with the computer have affected the teaching–learning process in schools and have made it much more feasible to customize the educational process for all children, including the gifted and talented.

Gifted individuals are as different from one another in personality as they are from those nongifted (Barron & Harrington, 1981; Bloom, 1985; Dellas & Gaier, 1970; Janos & Robinson, 1985), and many are unconventional in their needs, emotions, interests, attitudes, and values. A unique pattern of personality characteristics in individuals who are gifted in a certain domain is often evident when they are very young. For example, those gifted in sports might report a learning style preference for physical mobility, art-gifted people might prefer tactile, hands-on activities, and those who are gifted in social leadership might prefer involvement in personal–social groups. These are examples of the wide variety of learning style differences that characterize gifted learners with different focuses of interests and abilities. These differences are frequently a recipe for trouble in school and a major cause of talent loss. People who are more conventional in their interests, abilities, and learning styles generally do better in the formal school setting than those who deviate from the norm. By definition, talented and gifted people are frequently unconventional in these respects.

What we have learned thus far about the importance of home learning preferences in customizing education in and out of school for nongifted children is certainly applicable to gifted children. Most of the knowledge about the learning styles of the gifted until recently dealt with learning in the school setting, with little research conducted on home learning styles. Accordingly, this work is summarized with the expectation that some of the conclusions about the value of customizing the teaching–learning process for gifted students in the classroom will generalize to the performance of homework outside the classroom.

GIFTEDNESS, LEARNING STYLE, HOMEWORK MOTIVATION AND PREFERENCE

To the best of our knowledge, only two empirical studies of home learning motivation and preference of gifted learners have been conducted (the study conducted for this book; Ohayon, 1999). This section briefly summarizes the findings of the two studies on homework motivation and preference in gifted learners and those of studies on the in-school learning styles of gifted and talented students and suggests possible applications and future research directions.

School Learning Styles of Gifted and Talented Learners

In the 1980s, Dunn and her collaborators conducted a series of studies on learning styles of high IQ-type gifted students. They found that high

IQ children had a pattern of learning style preferences that was different from that of the others. For example, high IQ learners were found to be more persistent (Dunn & Price, 1980; Griggs & Price, 1980; Price, Dunn, Dunn, & Griggs, 1981; Ricca, 1983) and more highly motivated (Cody, 1983; Cross, 1982; Dunn & Price, 1980; Griggs & Price, 1980; Price et al., 1981). They strongly preferred to learn by themselves rather than with others (Cross, 1982; Griggs & Price, 1980; Price et al., 1981; Ricca, 1983), unless the others were equally high-achieving peers (Perrin, 1984, 1985). High IQ children preferred independent learning (Stewart, 1981; Wasson, 1980) and a formal, rather than informal, learning environment (Price et al., 1981), and were especially opposed to learning directly from the teacher.

Previous research has demonstrated that matching the features of the learning environment in school with the students' preferred learning style yields beneficial results, and the mismatch detrimental ones. One may ask whether this conclusion applies equally to gifted students, or are they able to compensate on their own and minimize the detrimental features of the mismatch? One answer to this question is found in a study investigating gifted and nongifted students who were matched and mismatched for learning alone versus learning with peers (Perrin, 1984, 1985). The results clearly indicated that matching was better for gifted as well as nongifted students. DeBello (1985) found similar results with eighth graders on matching for learning with peers versus learning with the teacher. We conclude that gifted learners, like their nongifted same-age peers, also benefit from instructional procedures that are congruent with their learning style characteristics.

Research on learning style in schools went international with the translation of the LSI (Dunn et al., 1987) into eight other languages and its administration to approximately 6,000 gifted and nongifted adolescents in Grades 7 through 12 in nine countries (Brazil, Canada, Egypt, Greece, Guatemala, Israel, Korea, Philippines, and the United States). Milgram et al., (1993) reported the complex findings of this large-scale international study in detail. As part of the international study, Milgram and Price (1993) examined the learning styles of 985 Israeli adolescents identified as gifted and nongifted in at least one of 14 domains. The domains were as follows: general intellectual ability as indicated by high IQ scores, specific intellectual ability as indicated by high grades in school subjects (Hebrew literature, Hebrew language, mathematics, and English [a foreign language in Israel]), high-divergent thinking ability, and high creative attainments in 11 specific domains (science, mathematics, computer, social leadership, dance, music, art, literature, foreign languages, drama, and sport). Adolescents were classified as either gifted or nongifted in the specific creative talent domains on the basis of the TAAI (Milgram, 1990). The learning style components that were found to discriminate (marked with the letter D) between the gifted and nongifted groups in each of the 14 domains are presented in Table 6.1. The letter D marked with an asterisk indicates that the gifted group had a higher score than the nongifted group on the learning style.

There were two sets of important findings. First, gifted students differed in learning style from nongifted on many domains. Second, gifted students in one domain differed in learning style from gifted students in another. For example, learners gifted in science reported a different profile of learning style preferences than those gifted in mathematics, dance, or sport. The most remarkable finding in the analyses of the 14 domains was that no two patterns of learning style were the same (e.g., science-gifted vs. art-gifted vs. sports-gifted, etc.) among the adolescents of the nine countries.

In light of the relationship between in-school and out-of-school learning (Hong, Milgram, & Perkins, 1995; Perkins & Milgram, 1996), these findings on in-school learning preferences may be helpful to teachers and parents in individualizing homework assignments. These data will help parents recognize the motivation and preferences of their children and become more tolerant and considerate of these features of their children's behavior. Space limitations do not allow a detailed analysis of the learning style profile of each of the 14 gifted and nongifted groups. We selected two gifted group profiles, the one high IQ-gifted and the other, highly creative-thinking gifted to illustrate how these data may be interpreted.

The learning style of the high IQ gifted group (some of who received high grades in school and some of whom did not) was compared with the learning style of the academically gifted (some of whom had high IQ and some of whom did not). When compared to the academically nongifted, the academically gifted were more highly teacher-motivated, did not report the need for freedom to move about the classroom while learning, and cited a preference to learn visually. The pattern of preferences of academically gifted learners is clearly consonant with the kinds of attitudes that lead to successful performance in most conventional classrooms. By contrast, consider the learning style preferences reported by high IQ-gifted learners as a group, bearing in mind that only some of them receive high grades in school. They reported stronger preferences for independent learning without same-age peers or adult authority figures present. They are less motivated by parents and teachers, less conforming, have a higher preference for visual- and kinesthetic-oriented learning, and prefer sound over silence when studying. These learning preferences do not match the conventional situation in most classrooms and provide a possible explanation for a particularly perplexing and disturbing problem. The academic failure of many highly able students may well be the result of the conflict between their pre-

Table 6.1
Learning Style Components That Differentiate between Gifted and Nongifted Learners in Israel

Groups / Components	IQ	Academic Achievement	Creative Thinking	Science	Math	Computer	Social Leadership	Music	Art	Dance	Drama	Sport	Literature	Foreign Language
Motivation														
Source														
Self-Motivated	D	D*			D*	D		D		D	D			D*
Parent-Motivated	D	D		D	D		D	D	D					D*
Teacher-Motivated	D	D*		D*	D*	D*	D*	D*	D*	D*		D*		
Strength														
Persistence			D	D*	D	D				D*				D
Promptness	D			D*		D	D*			D*				D*
Preference														
Organizational														
Structure			D						D					D
Surroundings														
Sound	D*			D				D*	D*	D	D			D*
Light					D	D*	D*		D*	D*		D*	D	
Temperature	D*					D*	D*	D	D			D*	D	
Design			D	D	D*	D*				D				
Perceptual-Physical														
Auditory	D*			D			D*				D*	D*		
Visual	D	D*					D		D					
Tactile	D*		D*	D*	D*	D*	D*	D*	D*	D*	D*	D	D	
Kinesthetic	D*		D*	D*	D*	D	D*	D*	D*	D	D*	D	D*	
Intake	D*			D*	D*		D*	D*	D*			D*	D*	
Mobility	D	D		D	D	D		D					D	
Interpersonal														
Alone-Peers	D	D	D	D*		D*							D	D
Authority Figures	D	D	D	D	D	D		D*	D	D*			D	D

* Gifted higher than nongifted

ferred learning styles and the learning situations in which they find themselves.

A second finding of the Milgram et al. (1993) international study on high creative-thinking learners also highlights the explanatory power of the learning style pattern of gifted students. High creative thinkers in the study differed from their low creative-thinking same-age peers on a number of components. They reported stronger tactile and kinesthetic preferences, suggesting that they would profit from active involvement in experiential learning as well as from the opportunity to explore and handle a wide variety of materials as they learn. They preferred less structure in their school tasks, which would allow them to define, interpret, and work on the tasks in various ways. They also preferred an informal learning environment, possibly one containing easy chairs and other soft furniture. On the other hand, they reported themselves to be less persistent and less comfortable in the presence of authority figures than did the comparison low creative-thinking group. These findings substantiate some widespread views about creative-thinking children.

Price and Milgram (1993) drew a number of conclusions that have worldwide implications because they were based on a large international sample:

1. Clear cross-cultural differences occur in the learning styles of gifted adolescents among the nine cultures and significant differences of learning styles between gifted and nongifted learners within each culture.

2. Young people gifted in the same domain shared some learning style preferences even though they lived in very different cultures. Science-gifted students were more persistent and showed a stronger preference for learning through their tactile sense than were their science-nongifted peers across five of the nine countries studied. Students gifted in social leadership expressed a kinesthetic preference when learning, that is, they enjoyed active participation tasks, when compared to their corresponding nongifted peers across five cultures.

3. The investigators combined gifted learners in all countries into a single group, regardless of domain, and compared them to a corresponding group of their nongifted peers. They found that gifted and talented students shared several learning style preferences. First, they preferred to learn more through tactile and kinesthetic preferences. Second, they preferred to learn alone rather than with their peers. These conclusions across countries and talent domains point to an unfortunate mismatch of student preferences and classroom realities. Gifted and talented adoles-

cents prefer to learn via tactile and kinesthetic modes, but study in classrooms that emphasize visual and auditory modes. They prefer to study alone, but are required to study in groups made up of their peers, even within the special education programs presumably designed for them.

The practical implications of these findings are of considerable importance.

Homework Motivation and Preferences of Gifted and Talented Learners

The effort to understand the homework motivation and preference of gifted and talented learners is at a very early stage. In the study conducted for this book, the HMPQ (Hong & Milgram, 1998) was administered to 126 fifth graders in Israel. The students' talent in science, leadership, and dance was assessed by 13, 12, and 10 items that tapped out-of-school activities in the respective domains taken from the TAAI (Milgram, 1998). Examples of such accomplishments include receiving an award for a science project (science), being chosen for a leadership position in a youth group (social leadership), and giving a solo dance performance (dance). Both the HMPQ and the TAAI were group administered in classrooms at the same time with no time limits. Both instruments possess high construct validity. Construct validity of the HMPQ was discussed in detail in chapter 2. The construct validity of the TAAI (including discriminant, predictive, and factorial validity) has been demonstrated in numerous studies (e.g., Hong & Milgram, 1996; Hong, Milgram, & Gorsky, 1995; Hong, Milgram, & Whiston, 1993; Hong, Whiston, & Milgram, 1993; Milgram & Hong, 1994; Milgram & Milgram, 1976).

The goal of the first part of the study was to investigate whether the HMPQ could discriminate between individuals talented in the domains of science, social leadership, and dance. These domains were chosen because of an a priori assumption that they would be associated with very different learning preference patterns. The HMPQ components that showed significant relationships with the activities and accomplishment scores in science, social leadership, and dance activity scores are presented in Table 2.4 (see chapter 2). The major findings and their possible explanations are presented briefly.

(1) Science-gifted students, compared with students gifted in the other two domains, were highly self-, parent-, and teacher-motivated when doing homework. Several explanations exist for these findings. First, students who are talented in science tend to be high academic achievers and build their achievements in science outside of school on the basis of

the knowledge they acquire in their science courses. Second, the motivational pattern associated with their homework is similar to the motivational pattern required to achieve scientific accomplishments. Interest in science is often inspired or encouraged by teachers or parents (e.g., support of teachers and of parents in devising the project, acquiring the equipment, and conducting the experiment); hence, the high standing on the science-gifted group in self-, teacher- and parent-motivation.

(2) The dance-talented group was very different. These students do not learn dance in school and there is no necessary match between the preferences relevant to dance and after-school homework assignments. Hence, they may be less motivated to complete their homework, whatever the source of motivation—self, teachers, or parents.

(3) The social leadership group was high in parent- and teacher-motivation, possibly because of their tendency to strive to satisfy the people around them. They were also highest in persistence in homework completion, a motivational component that is very important if one is to function in a leadership role. No explanation exists as to why these students were not higher in self-motivation, except that, like the dance-talented group, a poor match may exist between the interests and skills associated with social leadership and those associated with doing the conventional homework assignments.

(4) Talented students in all three groups preferred to learn through the tactile channel, that is, by hands-on learning activities that afford the opportunity to manipulate materials. Those talented in the science and social leadership areas preferred to learn via the auditory channel, whereas the dance-talented group preferred the visual channel. The preference of the science-talented students for auditory learning is not easily interpretable. By contrast, the social leaders' auditory preference reflects their numerous interactions with other people that involve talking and listening. By the same token, a visual preference serves dance-gifted individuals well in their need to observe how others dance in a very systematic way and to be able to receive instructions from teachers who model the dance routines they will be required to master.

(5) The preference of organizing homework assignments in the same order was related to science-talented students only. Dance- and social leadership-talented students preferred to do their homework in different places and not in the same place all the time. As expected, leadership-talented individuals preferred doing their homework with peers.

These findings are consistent with some of the preconceived notions about the different homework preferences that might characterize learners whose abilities are more closely associated with disciplined and systematic efforts versus those of their peers whose talents are more creative and divergent.

The Disparity between Learning Preferences and Learning Requirements

As might be expected, people do not always get what they want, and students' learning preferences are not always honored in the classroom and in the home. In recent research (presented in chapter 3), Hong and Milgram (1999) found that many learners experience a gap between how they prefer to do their homework and how they actually do it. These investigators examined the effect on homework achievement of the disparity between preferred homework conditions (how they would have preferred to do their homework and the actual conditions in which they did their homework. Results of the study indicated that (a) just as there are many students who do not learn in school according to their individual preferences, many do not do their homework according to these preferences either, and (b) certain indices of homework motivation and preference were related to homework achievement and attitude in nongifted learners (see chapter 5).

Ohayon (1999) investigated whether the disparity between preferred and actual home learning style reported earlier for nongifted learners was obtained in high and low creative-thinking children as well. She also examined the relationship of the preferred–actual gap to homework achievement. Some disparities were found only in children with low creative thinking. Interestingly enough, the specific disparities found in low creative-thinking learners were easily remedied if parents made simple accommodations such as providing more light, permitting their children to move around while doing homework, and allowing children to shift from one place to another in the home as they did their homework. A corresponding preferred–actual disparity was not found in children of high creative-thinking ability. They were apparently able to find ways to persuade their parents to accede to their preferences or to find other ways to have their preferences met. Creative-thinking learners, by definition, are able to generate more unusual and high-quality solutions to a wide variety of problems that occur in life. How they handled the circumstances in which they did their homework is simply another example of their problem-solving skills.

Taken together, the results of studies in three different cultures (the United States, Korea, and Israel) indicated that there is a gap between how children in the fifth and seventh grades prefer to do their homework and how they actually do it. Participants in these studies were relatively young. Whether or not the preferred–actual disparity obtains in students older than those investigated so far and in additional cultures as well is worthy of further investigation.

It is important for parents to realize that accommodating to the homework preferences of their children is worthwhile because it contributes to the academic quality of the homework assignments themselves and it improves children's attitudes toward homework. Ohayon (1999) computed a score that reflected the disparity between the preferred and actual conditions under which children did their homework and found a correlation of $-.29$ between this score and perceived achievement on homework. In other words, the greater the gap indicating low parent awareness, the lower the achievement. The same relationship between this gap and homework achievement was found for the following six homework preference components: light $(-.23)$, design $(-.28)$, parent-motivated $(-.22)$, structure $(-.23)$, order $(-.25)$, intake $(-.26)$, all $ps <$ .05. The negative relationship between the preferred–actual gap and achievement was found to be the same for high as well as for low creative-thinking learners. These findings should provide incentive for parents to increase understanding of their child's homework motivation and preferences and to accommodate the actual conditions under which homework is done to these preferences. These data were obtained only from the children themselves and not from their parents. The next step in investigating the preferred–actual homework gap in gifted and talented students and its implications for achievement and attitude is to gather data on parental awareness and support.

In conclusion, an important caveat is in order. As we attempt to generalize about the in-school and out-of-school learning preferences of gifted students, we should always bear in mind that every gifted individual has a unique personal learning style. The findings reported here on learning style of gifted learners, are valid for gifted learners as a group, but do not apply to any single gifted learner. These findings do, however, have implications for policy. They are relevant to almost all aspects of policy in gifted education: identification, curriculum, and instruction. Policy changes are urgently needed that reflect the multidimensional character of giftedness. Individualized learning style-oriented instruction in schools merits serious attention as an alternative to current group-oriented practices. By the same token, the findings have implications for parents and teachers. Even at this early stage of research on the topic, it is clear that teachers and parents working together can create homework assignments and the environment in which to do them that will be more productive in terms of the school's achievement goals, and a more satisfying and enjoyable experience for parents and children.

PART III

HOMEWORK STRATEGIES AND INTERVENTIONS

7

Solving Homework Problems

ADAPTIVE INSTRUCTION

Educators and parents often wonder why some students learn easily while others struggle. There are many factors that contribute to this situation. Students' aptitudes for learning, their motivation to learn, and their styles or preferences for how to learn are some of the major variables that impact on the learning processes and produce individual differences in learning rates. Another factor, which has not been a major topic in this volume is learning outcomes or tasks. Various tasks require different thought processes, resulting in an interaction of learner variables with learning outcomes (Jonassen & Grabowski, 1993). This volume focuses on a specific learner variable—*learning style* or *learning preference*. The two terms are used synonymously. However, the term *learning style* has been used extensively by Dunn and Dunn in their work on children's preferred learning environment in the classroom, and the term *learning preference* is used here to refer to children's preferred learning environment when doing their homework.

That each child has his or her own learning preferences is no longer a subject for debate. There is disagreement, however, as to whether efforts should be made to change or expand students' learning preferences to conform to classroom instructions, or to adapt instructions to match students' preferred modes of learning (i.e., teach to students' strengths). Some educators may disagree as to how to treat these learning differences in classrooms and in home learning situations, but all appreciate the impact of these differences on effective learning. Jeter and Chauvin (1982) illustrated well the need for accommodating individual differences in education: "Educators are keenly aware that each student possesses unique needs, interests, and abilities, and that each child should have an opportunity to pursue an effective instructional program at a pace that is challenging and interesting" (p. 2).

Varying Views on Adaptive Instruction

According to Kolb (1984), learning style develops as a consequence of heredity factors, previous learning experiences, and the demands of the present environment. As a result, most people develop learning styles or preferences that emphasize certain learning abilities over others. For example, students who are used to hearing lectures in class may develop an auditory preference in learning, although they might otherwise have preferred other modalities. Cornett (1983), Davidman (1981), Hong and Suh (1995), and Reid (1987) found that learning preferences—even although relatively stable—do change in individuals over time due to maturation, cultural, and environmental stimuli. Those investigators who contend that much of learning styles is biologically imposed on humans are encouraged by research findings that learning styles are immutable and remain consistent, regardless of the subject taught or the nature of the learning environment (Copenhaver, 1979; Kalous, 1990; Restak, 1979).

Some learning style proponents (e.g., Dunn and Dunn) represent the view that children should be taught initially through their strengths. According to Dunn and Dunn's model (1972), if a student is to have the best opportunity to learn, individual styles must be identified and instructional strategies congruent with these styles must be used. These proponents favor adapting the instructions, changing the learning environment, and not retraining the child. They underscore the value of individual differences in style variations, suggesting that emphasis be given to a variety of learning environments multiple resources, variable instructional methodologies, and flexible teaching to accommodate these individual differences (Keefe, 1988).

Others advocate training people to actually change their cognitive profiles for coping with existing learning environments (e.g., Letteri, 1980). Believing that certain cognitive skills are more productive of school achievement than others it was recommended that learner skills be modified or augmented in order for learning to take place and that the schools' efforts should be directed toward the development of curricula based on task analysis (Jonassen & Grabowski, 1993; Keefe, 1988; Letteri, 1980). They contend that it is important to challenge the learner to learn new approaches that are not preferred, but are more efficient. As learners are exposed to a variety of educational experiences, they learn to adapt to a variety of instructional methods and styles (Messick, 1976). As indicated earlier, providing only auditory forms of instruction compels learners to develop auditory skills. Thus, the two approaches discussed so far provide opposite notions about adaptation: Whereas the former requires that instruction adapt to learner preferences, the latter requires the learner to adapt to the instruction and learning environment.

A third approach combines the previous two approaches; that is, recognizing learners' individual differences as well as learners' need to adapt to the environment (DeBello, 1990; Gregorc, 1985). Although learners try to use their preferred modes of learning, if the learning environments or instructions demand otherwise, they can be encouraged to use other learning modes. Although at first, learning may not be as efficient as when they used their preferred learning modes, encouragement will lead them to learn new ways of learning. This approach emphasizes matching instruction to individual preferences, especially when learning involves new or difficult materials, and supplementing students' preferences with varied instructional strategies and materials to expand students' learning styles. Students who are mature and capable benefit from this combined strategy more than either of the other two approaches alone.

Assumptions of This Book

We acknowledge the merits as well as the practical problems in implementing the more learner-centered flexible approaches in the instruction and learning that take place in the school. We are convinced that our homework motivation and preference model, with its emphasis on accommodating students' individual learning preferences, is especially appropriate for children who are having difficulties in learning in school or at home. Considering the feasibility problems and resource limitations of the adaptive instruction approach, we contend that individualized homework treatment be applied first to those students experiencing homework problems while using student learning preferences, and then to include the whole class by establishing a homework intervention system.

When a child is experiencing the difficulty in homework completion, their preferred way of learning and studying should be accommodated at home ("matching to the student's preferences"). If the child is still experiencing homework difficulties with this environmental accommodation, another style or strategy might be introduced with the anticipation that it may be more effective than the one they currently use ("supplementing the student's preference"). The supplementing strategy could be accomplished, for example, by applying the information from research findings indicating particular styles or preferences having strong associations with high achievement and positive attitude toward homework. This approach should go hand in hand with the constant checks to determine whether the introduction of a new strategy has been effective and successful or whether there is a need to introduce still another strategy in search of the best way for a particular learner to do his or her homework.

Like S. Sims and Sims (1995), we do not argue that learning preferences are more important than other learning needs or than alternative processes for learning. However, we insist that by accommodating students' learning preferences, it is likely that students' learning potentials will be actualized. We contend that when teachers adapt homework requirements and circumstances to individual learners, they help them complete their homework and learn more from doing it, and thereby enhance their school achievement. A few homework studies have found increased student achievement as a consequence of permitting this match of student home learning preferences and environmental cues and supports (e.g., Clark-Thayer, 1987; Hong, Tomoff et al., 2000).

LEARNING STYLE INTERVENTION

The Need for Learning Style Intervention

Although a program of adaptive instructions accommodating student learning styles is considered helpful in improving student learning, it has been rarely implemented in schools (see the examples of the intervention studies presented later). L. J. Campbell (1990) indicated, in his literature review and survey of elementary teachers, that the reasons for failure to implement this kind of program were several: overly large class size (Oakes, 1989), poor administrative leadership and lack of support, inadequate teacher training, and poorly developed learning style instruments (Curry, 1987, 1990). The survey highlighted several deficiencies in teacher training: First, it is often too short, and second, the teachers' understanding of learning styles is not extensive enough to apply to their classroom practice.

Some schools have embraced the learning style concept and have begun to introduce it in their school system through in-service training. Learning Styles Network, directed by Rita Dunn at the Center for the Study of Learning and Teaching Styles at St. John's University, has been a major force in this endeavor. Although the teachers who have undergone in-service training realize the benefits of individualized, student-centered learning and teaching approaches, there has been little follow-up with teachers on the application of what they learned in in-service training and what they actually do in their classrooms (Abbott-Shim, 1990; Guskey, 1990). Because these individualized programs require substantial resources, they must receive the complete support of the educational administration. For learning style interventions to be successful, administrators must not only understand and accept the concepts of learning styles, they must also support teachers in changing the way they teach and in preparing the instructional materials and homework assignments that match each individual student's strengths.

In summary, these individualized programs will be successful if certain conditions are met, including administrators' support, appropriate guidelines for implementing the programs, teachers' awareness that no single method can meet the challenge set by the wide range of differences in student learning preference that exist in the classroom, and teachers' willingness to change their teaching strategies. Teachers must ascertain students' learning preferences to adopt and develop the adaptive instruction and homework approaches and assess those learning situations where supplementing a student's learning preference with other approaches is beneficial to the student.

Research on Learning Style Intervention

A number of studies demonstrate that the matching of student learning styles and learning environment improves student achievement. The theoretical basis for this research is based on Hunt's (1975) concept on person–environment interaction in learning. Student learning in school is a function of student characteristics (e.g., gender, aptitude, learning style) and environment (e.g., instructional strategy, curriculum, classroom environment). Similarly, student learning at home is a function of student characteristics (e.g., home learning preferences) and environment (e.g., home environment, types and quality of homework assignments).

Although full implementation of learning style applications in school systems is still rare, numerous small-scale in-school learning style intervention studies have been conducted. Most studies with elementary and secondary students have used the LSI (Dunn et al., 1979, 1981, 1984, 1987, 1989a). Dunn and her associates reported that research with the LSI has been extensive, with students from kindergarten through college with various levels of academic proficiency, including gifted, average, underachieving, at risk, dropout, special education, and vocational and industrial arts populations. Many of these studies have compared the effects on achievement of matching versus mismatching the learning style elements with instructional strategies, and reported positive effects for matching strategies (e.g., Dunn et al., 1995).

Studies with adult learners also support the contention that learning is more efficient when students are presented with information that is matched to their learning styles (Boulmetis & Sabula, 1996; Kolb, 1984; R. Sims & Sims, 1995). Hayes and Allinson (1993) conducted an extensive review of the matching hypothesis on specific learning style variables proposed by Kolb (1984), Witkin (1976), and others (e.g., Kagan, Moss, & Sigel, 1963), and concluded that, notwithstanding some mixed findings, there is a basis for suggesting that learning style is a more important and influential characteristic of learners than some of the other well-researched individual learners' characteristics (e.g., aptitude).

Research on Homework Style Intervention

Just as students bring individual differences into the classroom learning situation, they also bring individual differences in the form of different competence levels and learning preferences to their homework assignments. Uniform homework assignments do not address student variation. To meet the individual differences in doing homework, homework assignments must take into consideration students' learning preferences and their levels of acquired study skills and competence in homework materials (Epstein, Polloway, Foley, & Patton, 1993; Rosenberg, 1995). Although some students do well with any kind of homework assignment, many are not equipped to do some or all homework assignments well. These students will not learn much from doing homework unless there is a match between the level of the assignment and their level of competence in doing the assignment and a corresponding match between their learning preferences and environmental supports at home.

Some of the difficulties in implementing a homework intervention program were noted in Hong, Tomoff et al. (2000). Parents showed interest in the intervention when they were contacted by phone or at the parent–teacher conferences. However, when the project was actually in progress, they were not as accommodating as they previously said they would be. This may have been because the students in this study were not identified as having homework problems or because parents and students may not believe that accommodating conditions to learning preferences increases academic achievement. Nevertheless, there were two positive consequences of the intervention:

1. When treatment and control groups were compared following the intervention, students exposed to the intervention perceived themselves doing their homework better than students not exposed to the intervention.
2. Students who actually applied their strong preferences in doing homework had more positive attitudes toward homework than those who did not.

These findings based on students without special homework problems suggest that students with homework problems who have even stronger incentives for applying the adaptive homework approach will do so, to their advantage, thereby improving their homework performance.

Another study that indirectly supports the importance of the adaptive learning approach to homework was done by Marino (1993). Incoming freshmen at an all-boys high school in Brooklyn, New York were given the LSI (Dunn et al., 1987), and their teachers were given in-house training in the model's practical features, followed by appropriate information and feedback to students and parents in workshop sessions designed for them. The findings were that use of the LSI profile by teachers and parents assisted students in dealing with homework in a "preferential way," thus making significant differences in their learning.

These studies suggest that accommodating students' home learning preferences by manipulating environmental conditions at home will make homework completion more meaningful and productive. This endeavor requires a commitment by classroom teachers and the continuing support of parents, and if these are provided, students may acquire a more positive attitude toward homework and learn from doing their homework.

SOLVING HOMEWORK PROBLEMS

Teachers and most parents and students believe that doing homework increases school achievement and helps students take responsibility for themselves. One of the major frustrations in school is the failure of many students to complete their homework assignments because they are not willing or able to do so. Nevertheless, teachers depend on homework to fulfill a variety of functions because they believe that it is effective in enhancing student achievement.

To achieve positive results in homework and home learning, teamwork by all three parties—students, teachers, and parents—is necessary. Classroom teachers assign and evaluate the homework, and students do the homework. However, the homework is done at home, where teachers cannot exercise control, but parents can and do (Bryan & Sullivan-Burstein, 1997; Olympia, Sheridan, & Jenson, 1994). For example, teamwork can involve teachers conveying their assessment of a student's home learning preference at a parent–teacher conference. At the meeting, the student, teacher, and parent discuss the student's homework motivation and preferences and work as a team to determine the best home learning environment.

According to Jenson, Sheridan, Olympia, and Andrews (1995), home–school collaboration, based on consistency and coordination between parents and teachers, is essential to increasing the effectiveness of homework, maintaining work habits, and generalizing from these homework outcomes to the other academic outcomes. The home–school relationship may best be conceptualized as a partnership, in which parents, teachers, and students share the responsibility for attaining educational objectives. To enhance the effectiveness of homework, it is necessary for teachers, parents, and students to share various tasks such as identifying homework problems, assessing home learning preferences, developing an effective homework intervention to be used across home and school settings, and systematically monitoring the effects of the intervention on improvement of homework and school performance. Intervention programs emphasizing teamwork are provided in chapter 8. The following section discusses the role of parents, teachers, and students in improving homework outcomes.

PARENTAL INVOLVEMENT IN HOMEWORK

Homework is a part of the lives of most families with school children. Homework might be experienced as either an unwelcome intrusion by school assignments into the student's personal world, or an extension of enriching and meaningful schoolwork into personal life. When Reetz (1990/1991) involved parents in her homework study, the homework questionnaire evoked strong reactions. Some parents were very much in favor of the assignment of homework, indicating that all good teachers assigned homework; whereas others felt it was destroying what little family time they had left in today's society. The quote from a parent, "Homework has dominated and ruined our lives for the past 8 years," in Bryan and Sullivan-Burstein (1997) indicates the extent to which an inordinate focus and inappropriate monitoring of children's homework can cause problems in family life.

In general, parents are willing to help with their children's homework when they believe they are needed, and do so even if it is a frequent source of conflict between them and their children. When surveying parents on six types of involvement in their children's education, the Family Center at Johns Hopkins University found that respondents were uninterested in regular school visits or in participating in policy and decision making, but were eager to help their children at home (Hollifield, 1995).

Although involving parents in their children's homework can increase the value of homework for the children (Walberg, 1984), parents generally are not asked how the partnership between home and school can be strengthened, and they often feel confused about how they can best assist their children with homework (Swap, 1993). However, when parents were contacted by the teachers regarding their children's home learning preferences, they were pleased to be asked and to be involved (Hong, Tomoff et. al., 2000). Students also believe they do better in school when their parents help them with homework, although they also report mixed perceptions about how much they enjoyed working with their parents.

Many perceptions focused on the extent to which parents either facilitated or confused the student's understanding of homework concepts
and the positive or negative affect associated with parent–child interactions (Balli, 1998). These findings caution that the way in which parents
are involved in homework makes a difference, and it can be either positive in its influence or negative and damaging to achievement and
attitudes (Cooper, 1989a; Epstein et al., 1993). Effective parental involvement in the homework process should be a focus for homework intervention studies.

Increasing Parental Involvement: Communication Problems

Homework involves parents in the school process, thus enhancing
their appreciation of education. Parental involvement is beneficial for
children's education, thus it is unfortunate that many parents are reluctant to be involved (Blackfelner & Ranallo, 1998). Reasons for this reluc-
tance included parents' fear of school, parents' lack of time, parents' lack
of transportation, and parents' embarrassment about their own education level. On the other hand, parents want a communication system that
allows them to learn more about curriculum and pedagogy; their own
role and the teacher's expectations of their children; individualization of
homework assignments and nontraditional homework assignments such
as hands-on homework (Kay, Fitzgerald, Paradee, & Mellencamp, 1995).
Without proper channels of communication, parents will not become involved at all or terminate their involvement soon after they initiate it.

Efforts have been made to facilitate teacher–parent communication
(Epstein et al., 1997). For instance, one study solicited recommendations
for solving communication problems that arise when homework is assigned to students with mild disabilities in general education classes. The
recommendations included creating time and opportunity (use of technology and conferences in the evening), increasing knowledge about
means of communication (necessary information about communication
and ways of communicating information regularly), attitudes and abilities (positive communication and increased student responsibility), by-
pass (strategies to reduce the need for communication) (Jayanthi,
Bursuck, Epstein, & Polloway, 1997). Various communication approaches
can be utilized according to the student and family needs, including
telephone conferences, parent–teacher conferences, email, special events,
open house programs, daily homework journal, homework checklists
that involve the student, parent, and teacher, and other printed means
of communication such as class newsletter, written comments, and note-
books.

In summary, parents want their children to learn. If they do not know
what their children are doing in school and what they are required to

do at home, parents cannot become effectively involved in their children's education. Some parents are not aware that their children are doing badly until parent–teacher conference time or until they receive report cards. When teachers make efforts to communicate with parents, parents generally support the teachers' requests. Effective communication about teacher expectations and other aspects of life in the classroom will enable parents to become involved in planning and helping their children.

Parental Involvement in Homework Process

Educators recognize parent cooperation in the homework process as a necessary factor in making homework more effective. When parents provide a suitable place for children to do the homework, the requisite supplies, and their encouragement and assistance on homework completion, they contribute greatly toward this end (Bryan & Sullivan, 1995). Effective parental involvement is not easily achieved. It is not uncommon that parents and their children disagree about when, where, or how they should be doing homework (Hong & Lee, 1999a). Martin and Potter (1998) indicated that often parents are unaware of how their children most effectively learn and study. Parents themselves, when they were students, had been told to do their homework in certain ways (e.g., do homework as soon as they arrive home from school; sit at a desk or table with a bright light; no background music; no food). This is not necessarily what is best for many young people. By allowing children to do their homework based on their preferred homework style, it is possible to change their attitude toward homework and to improve homework achievement. Students can complete their homework with much less stress and may even enjoy doing it.

Patton (1995) provided recommendations on how parents can best participate in the homework process. These are presented here together with our comments:

1. Serve in a supportive role in reinforcing what is taught in school, instead of teaching new academic skills.

2. Receive training, if possible, to increase the ability to assist their children. An example of parent training is provided in chapter 8.

3. Create a home environment that is conducive to doing homework.

4. Encourage and reinforce student effort. Although children generally appreciate their parents' encouragement, it is especially important for students who are parent-motivated. However, parents should avoid creating situations in which they are con-

stantly monitoring their child's work and making excessive corrections. This is especially detrimental to students who prefer not to have authority figures around when doing homework.

5. Maintain ongoing involvement. Parents need to be involved early on and stay involved over time as long as students appreciate their supervision. When students are motivated to do homework and are responsible in completing it, the level of supervision should be reduced and parents should trust their children to do the required work. However, in many instances, without long-term interest in and interaction with their child's homework, parents can expect that the original problems about homework will recur.

6. Communicate parents' own views about homework to school personnel.

TEACHERS' HOMEWORK STRATEGIES AND ADAPTATION

Research on homework effectiveness has been inconclusive partly because different mediating variables were included in the various studies (Cooper & Nye, 1994; Corno, 1996). Nevertheless, because some studies find that homework raises school achievement (e.g., Walberg et al., 1985), most educators regard it as an important instructional tool or means to enhance student achievement and academic skills (Frith, 1991; Mims, Harper, Armstrong, & Savage, 1991). Specifically, teachers use homework to increase the amount of time students spend on academic tasks, promote study habits, review skills, individualize instruction, provide additional practice, and involve parents in the educational process (Alleman & Brophy, 1991; Cooper & Nye, 1994; Gajria & Salend, 1995).

When teachers prepare and carefully plan homework assignments that are appropriate for the skill, attention, and motivation levels of students, these assignments achieve their goals (Cooper & Nye, 1994). For example, effective teachers may prepare homework assignments for individual students, deciding on types and amount of homework appropriate. This section discusses teacher awareness of student and personal learning preferences, the impact of inclusive education on homework, and adaptive homework utilizing individual differences in children's aptitudes and learning preferences.

Teacher Awareness of Student and Personal Learning Preferences

There is an apparent need to address how to provide homework assignments for students with homework difficulties. Both preservice and in-service teachers need to be trained on homework motivation and preference so they can individualize assignments. Teachers with formal training on how to use homework reported fewer obstacles to its implementation, viewed it as more important, and advocated its more frequent use (Cooper & Nye, 1994; Heller, Spooner, Anderson, & Mims, 1988). Unfortunately, most general education teachers are taught very little about effective homework practices at the preservice level (Pribble, 1993). Without adequate teacher training, poor homework quality and management results. Teacher training, both at the preservice and in-service levels should provide the proper design and use of assignments including how to adapt them according to individual student learning preferences.

L. J. Campbell (1990) investigated teacher awareness of various learning styles and strategies and found that teachers in his study could not recall any leading learning style models or instruments. Although some of the teachers remembered seeing in their professional journals articles about learning styles, they did not seem to pursue the topic further or to incorporate the concept into their teaching. Pettigrew and Buell (1989) also found that neither experienced nor preservice teachers accurately diagnosed the learning styles of their students.

This lack of awareness of learning styles in instruction and assessment methods has been recognized as one of the probable causes of poor student achievement (e.g., Mills & Stevens, 1998). Students in learning environments that utilize learning styles different than their own are placed at a disadvantage. If teachers recognize that instructional strategies are not equally effective for students with different learning preferences, possess the diagnostic skills to identify students' learning preferences, and apply them in school and home learning, students will have the opportunity to fully use their learning potential and consequently, their achievement will rise.

It is not unusual to observe teachers presenting the class with content and teaching materials based on the teacher's personal preference of learning. Dunn (1990) indicated that educators tend to utilize a single approach to all students, expecting students to achieve in any kind of learning environment, stressing conformity, and disregarding individual learning preferences. Thus, students whose learning preferences match those of the teacher seem to focus better on class activities and are usually high achievers (B. Campbell, 1991; Wuthrick, 1990). To be an effective educator, teachers need to devise diverse approaches for classroom instruction and homework that accommodate the individual strengths of all their students.

Inclusive Education and Homework

Increasingly more students with LD and emotional disorders are being educated in general education classes full or part time (U.S. Department of Education, 1992). As the movement toward inclusion accelerates within public schools, homework will require increased attention. Bryan and Nelson (1994) and Epstein and colleagues (Epstein et al., 1993; Polloway et al., 1992) confirmed that teachers and parents reported significantly more homework-related difficulties for students with LD and behavioral disorders. For example, these students had more negative feelings than their peers toward homework, demonstrated low homework completion rates, expressed boredom and resistance to assignments, and perceived themselves as being less competent than their peers. Additionally, they tended to be less persistent, were more likely to procrastinate, and were less motivated, needed to be reminded, and preferred to learn from adults or have someone present in the room (Yong & McIntyre, 1992). However, children with LD have more favorable attitudes regarding homework when assignments are made in the context of a strong support system of teachers, parents, and peers (Frith, 1991; Nicholls, McKenzie, & Shufro, 1995).

The implication of these studies is that placement of these students in regular classes will likely exacerbate homework difficulties. As some of these homework difficulties are also found in low-achieving students in regular classrooms (Hong, 1998), concerns about homework practices are equally important. Parents of academically talented students also report that their children have homework problems, although these problems may not be at the same level as those facing nongifted students (Worrell, Gabelko, Roth, & Samuels, 1999).

Rosenberg (1995) found that homework, when planned, assigned, and implemented in a structured, responsible manner, can maximize the effectiveness of direct instruction sequences with LD students. He indicated that successful homework completion is contingent on an atmosphere in which doing homework is expected, valued, and rewarded. Making parents aware of the importance of homework and enlisting their help in the overall system is another critical component in making homework effective. Finally, students must demonstrate at least moderate acquisition of instructional material in order for homework to be effective. For children who are not learning material during classroom instruction, their time may be better spent in a more directive teaching situation where initial acquisition of the material could be facilitated through some alternative instructional method. These conclusions are also applicable to low-achieving regular students who have persistent homework problems.

These studies encourage educators to consider various factors that af-

fect homework completion when they apply the home learning preference approach. In the following section, we discuss various forms of
homework adaptation.

Homework Adaptation

Studies on teacher attitudes toward new teaching strategies indicate
that teachers are willing to consider innovations in their classes if they
perceive them to be reasonable and desirable (Polloway et al., 1995).

Homework adaptations come in various forms. They may be schoolwide homework policy changes, interventions involving parents (e.g.,
concerns about homework environment, communication strategies), adaptations in homework assignments themselves (e.g., structural change
by providing more specific homework assignments or providing more
homework choices; easier or more complex content), or adaptations
in homework instructions (e.g., detailed instructions on how to complete
homework) or in feedback strategies in response to successful or unsuc-
cessful completion of assignments (e.g., praise, various correction procedures).

If teachers identify students' learning preferences at home, they can
provide tailormade homework directions and homework assignments so
they can capitalize on students' strengths in doing homework. For example, a teacher may make adjustments in feedback strategies for a particular student (e.g., oral or written comments, reward) according to the
student's needs and especially whether the student is highly teacher-
motivated in doing homework. Chapters 9 and 10 provide detailed strategies for each homework motivation and preference component.

If one assumes that learning preferences are diagnosed accurately for
students, and that teachers accommodate the students' preferred styles
to the best of their ability, it is unlikely that there will be complete compatibility in learners' preferences and learning environment, especially
when class size is large. When one considers all of the possible individual
preferences that should be matched by various homework assignments,
the number of required homework alternatives is enormous. One of the
acceptable approaches for enhancing compatibility is to accommodate to
a component of the student's learning preferences. For example, the
teacher provides homework instructions using several delivery methods,
for example, speaking (auditory), writing on the board (visual), or hands-
on or role-playing (tactile or kinesthetic), or offers students a choice between structured and unstructured homework. If enough options are
provided, individual students will find a reasonable match between the
options they choose and their learning preferences.

In summary, it is important that teachers appreciate individual differences in learning preferences. They should be aware of their own pref-

erences as well as those of their students and they should communicate the results of their assessment to the students so that they will more clearly recognize their preferred way of learning and more quickly appreciate the compatibility between their preferences and the features of the environment. Additionally, teachers should make efforts to adjust instructional delivery and homework assignments to students' preferences as well as provide opportunities for students to develop and expand their learning style repertoire. Teachers should expand their teaching strategies and not merely rely on those strategies with which they are comfortable. They should realize that if they teach or assign homework in only the way with which they are comfortable, only some students will be well matched to the style.

The Common Denominator of Successful Homework

Before teachers adapt homework assignments to individual student learning preferences, they have a basic responsibility to create quality homework assignments. The following is a list of general principles on homework that can be applied by classroom teachers in enhancing the learning process:

1. Construction of good and meaningful assignments and proper use of homework are basic requirements for homework improvement (Cooper & Nye, 1994). Some necessary conditions for constructing good assignments are that teachers (a) recognize and inform the purpose of the homework assignment to students, (b) relate homework to academic objectives (e.g., class instructional objectives) and to nonacademic objectives (e.g., application of what is learned in homework to relevant issues and behaviors in students' lives) so students can appreciate the value of homework from their perspective, and (c) match the type of homework (e.g., to retain current learning or to acquire new learning) and difficulty level with the student's stages of learning (Patton, 1995; Paulu & Darby, 1998).

2. Teachers should be proficient in establishing an effective flow of assignments, prompt review, and appropriate grading and feedback about completion and accuracy of the submitted assignments (Cooper & Nye, 1994; Epstein et al., 1993; Heller et al., 1988; Mims et al., 1991; Swanson, 1992). Students benefit from constructive feedback on the quality of their efforts. Paschal et al. (1984) found that returning homework assignments with comments, grades, or both had greater effects on academic achievement than when individualized feedback was not given.

3. Students must have and must apply self-management techniques and basic study skills (Archer, 1988; Bryan & Sullivan-
Burstein, 1997; Shields & Heron, 1989; Trammel, Schloss, &
Alper, 1995). Many students need to learn study skills in order
to successfully complete homework and other schoolwork as
well. Sullivan and Bryan (1995) developed the Sequenced Study
Skills Program to teach (a) basic strategies such as identifying
a time and place for doing homework, having the necessary
materials, placing completed work in a secure place, and remembering to bring it to school; (b) metacognitive skills for monitoring the impact of distractions such as television viewing at a time
scheduled for doing homework, recognizing signs of fatigue and
lack of attention, and developing methods to cope with these
distracters and obstacles; and (c) specific study skills such as
taking notes, using strategies to increase reading comprehension,
and using mnemonics as memory helpers.

Other effective homework practices are discussed in chapter 9. Teachers and parents are advised to consult books and articles of advice on
helping children with homework (e.g., Bursuck, 1995; Epstein, 1998;
Hoover-Dempsey et al., 1995; Radencich & Schumm, 1997; Rosemond,
1990).

STUDENT ROLE IN HOMEWORK SUCCESS

Student Attitude Toward Homework

Surveys of elementary and secondary students have found that students generally feel that homework assignments are necessary and help
them improve their grades and do better on exams (Wood, 1987). Although some students prefer easy, simple, and short homework assignments, others prefer challenging work. The type of homework students
like also varies widely from routine textbook exercises or worksheets to
projects that require hands-on creative endeavors; some students dislike
and even resent boring, meaningless homework (Hong, Topham et al.,
2000).

In terms of adaptive homework assignments, elementary students in
special education tend to agree that it is appropriate to give different
homework assignments to different students; students in regular education classes tend less to agree with this arrangement (Bryan & Nelson,
1994; Nelson, Epstein, Bursuck, Jayanthi, & Sawyer, 1998). Special education students are well aware of their difficulties and justify tailoring
the difficulty of homework assignments to their ability; students in reg-

ular classes are less comfortable with this arrangement possibly because they think that all should work and compete on equal terms.

Bryan and Nelson (1994) also found that junior high students were more likely than elementary students to agree that homework is dull and boring. Junior high students also reported getting more homework and finding school more boring than elementary school students. These negative judgments of homework by students raise the question "Why?" Lack of feedback on work done was thought to exacerbate the situation.

A promising finding in a recent study (Hong, Tomaff et al., 2000) was that students in Grades 9 and 10 said they are responsible for doing their homework and are able to structure their homework environment as they wish, as compared to seventh graders. Developmental differences in personal and situational variables related to effective homework performance should be taken into consideration when attempting to individualize homework.

Students' Need for Understanding Personal Learning Preferences

Educators should recognize the responsibility of the student in the enhancement of learning (S. Sims & Sims, 1995). Students should have the opportunity to assess their own learning preferences and should be encouraged to diversify those preferences (Reid, 1987). Students' recognition of their own learning styles and preferences can help them make useful decisions about how they should go about doing their homework (e.g., which information to select and to process). Friedman and Alley (1984) suggested that teacher guidance can motivate students to identify and utilize their preferred learning styles to their advantage. Although many learning style experts propose that teachers accommodate learning style differences, Fleming and Mills (1992; cited in S. Sims & Sims, 1995) shifted the primary responsibility to the students themselves, although they did not absolve teachers of their responsibility.

A discussion with teachers or counselors followed by the assessment of learning preferences could help students understand their own likely approach to learning situations and use or modify the learning approach when conditions and preferences do not match. Because teachers are unable to accommodate each student's learning preferences due to many and diverse requirements of students and the limited physical resources in schools and homes, students themselves may be able to achieve a better match of learning setting and personal learning preferences if they are both aware of their preferences and are willing to extend their learning style repertoire and build an integrated learning style.

Students who are knowledgeable about their learning preferences are able to perceive many of them as potential strengths and to learn to compensate for those that may handicap them in given learning situations (Bauer, 1987; Silverman, 1989). There is an enlightening story of a ninth-grade student who worked to convince the school board to allow changes in the lighting so that his best friend would not be handicapped in learning because of his strong reaction to bright lights (Studd, 1995). This is an excellent example of a situation in which a student proactively used his implicit knowledge of learning preference to help his friend do better in school. As teachers assess students' learning preferences and discuss these findings with students, more students will do what this ninth grader did, for themselves or for their classmates. They will be more responsible for their own homework by virtue of the fact that they can exercise some control over their learning environment and learning assignments, and that this exercise of control will permit them to learn in ways with which they are most comfortable.

8

Homework Intervention: Focusing on Homework Motivation and Preference

UTILIZING THE HOMEWORK MOTIVATION AND PREFERENCE PROFILE (HMPP)

The development and validation of the Questionnaire HMPQ provides an individual HMPP in the six areas postulated in the conceptual model: motivational source, motivational strength, organizational, surroundings, perceptual-physical, and interpersonal preference. The information provided by this self-report instrument can be of use to students, teachers, and parents. The HMPP can provide learners with the opportunity to reflect on their own motivations and preferences about homework. They can acquire knowledge both of themselves as learners and about some of the complexities of the learning process (Jonassen & Grabowski, 1993). When asked what they thought of the homework preference information that they received, one common answer was that it helped them to look further into how they do the homework (Hong, Tomoff et al., 2000). The same instrument can be used with the teachers to increase awareness of their own preferences about learning and about those of their students. The instrument can also be used with parents, who can be asked to respond to the items as they observe how their child prefers to do homework. In this chapter, we briefly introduce how the HMPQ and HMPP can be utilized in enhancing learning or teaching conditions for students, teachers, and parents. These topics are elaborated further in later chapters.

Increasing Student Awareness of Individual Differences in Learning Preferences

A classroom teacher, school counselor, or school administrator could assess the individual students' homework motivation and preference. Depending on the school's commitment to and student involvement in the homework intervention program of our model, a single student or groups of students who show homework difficulties, or the entire class or even the whole school population can be included in the HMPQ assessment.

A teacher or counselor will share the individual HMPP with the participating students directly. At the individual meeting, the individual HMPP will be interpreted by the teacher or counselor in an effort to help the student become aware of his or her own preferences and to urge the student to accommodate his or her home learning preferences. Teachers can help students understand the different ways individuals learn by explaining the differences in learning preferences that exist among and within students, teachers, families, and people from other cultures. Disagreements between mother and father about how children should study can be offered to students as an illustration of how people differ in their opinions and perceptions about the best way to learn. The Motivation subscale can help students understand who motivates their homework and how prompt and persistent they are in homework completion. Of particular importance is that students will become more observant about whether their home learning environment matches their own preferred way of learning, and will begin to implement their own preferences at home based on knowledge of their HMPP.

Teachers' Use of Individual Students' HMPP in Homework Interventions

Many teachers have little knowledge about individual differences in learning styles, the diagnostic skills to identify learning styles, or do not know how to accommodate to students' learning preferences (e.g., L. J. Campbell, 1990; Mills & Stevens, 1998; Pettigrew & Buell, 1989; see chapter 7 for more). Teachers tend to use their own styles in teaching and often do not realize that some students have very different ways of learning and that learning in ways that are different from their preferences has negative effects on their academic achievement.

By becoming involved in the learning preference project, teachers will have the chance to learn more about the individual differences and how these differences can be accommodated to improve teaching and learning. Teachers themselves should complete the learning preference assessments in order to understand their own preferences. A comparison of students' and their own learning preferences will help teachers modify and expand their strategies and materials to improve the teaching–learning processes.

With the information on the HMPP, teachers will gain knowledge on what motivates individuals to do their homework (e.g., teacher- or parent-motivated), and the way they prefer studying at home, especially in the HMPQ components on which the teacher can have major influence (e.g., structure of homework assignments, homework that accommodates various perceptual strengths). The HMPP can be an excellent source for parent–teacher conferences, where teachers can share with parents the HMPP information and request their cooperation. The need for in-service training on this topic and specific intervention strategies are illustrated in chapter 7.

Parents' Use of HMPP in Understanding and Accommodating Home Learning Environment

Through the HMPP, parents can understand and respect the differences in the ways their children learn and study. Parents can use the information for designing the home environment to accommodate the child's needs for sound or quiet, bright or dim lighting, warm or cool temperature, and formal or informal seating design. Parents can help with these home environment features as well as with other dimensions of home learning preferences, such as organization, perceptual-physical, and interpersonal needs. For example, with parental understanding of the child's interpersonal preference, such as the need for studying with peers, parents may be willing to coordinate learning situations so the child's need is met.

Parents need to know the child's source of motivation (self, parent, or teacher) and whether the child needs to improve in promptness and persistence in doing homework. Parental knowledge on this information will assist in emphasizing the source of the motivation as well as in encouraging promptness and persistence.

As indicated earlier, more information regarding what students, parents, and teachers can do with the HMPP information are presented later in this chapter and in chapter 9. Teachers and parents should monitor whether the accommodations made based on the HMPP are helping students to do homework more successfully and to improve overall homework performance. Based on the observations, they can decide on the next step (e.g., supplementing the child's preferences), if deemed necessary.

HOMEWORK INTERVENTION: FOCUS ON STUDENT HOMEWORK PREFERENCES

Although homework problems are prevalent among students and impair learning and achievement (Anesko & O'Leary, 1982; Epstein et al., 1993), research on homework interventions to improve homework performance has been restricted to a small number of experimental and action research studies (e.g., Anderson, Bassett-Anderson, Gerretsen, Robilotta, 1997; Anliker, Aydt, Kellams, & Rothlisberger, 1997; Pierce, 1997; Rosenberg, 1995; Trammel et al., 1995).

Intervention studies focusing on home learning preferences are scarce. Future studies on this topic should involve classroom teachers and parents as major participants in training and intervention. These interventions are likely to be most effective for students having homework difficulties, but may also benefit students who are not having special difficulties by improving their attitudes toward homework and increasing how much they get out of doing it.

First Intervention: Involving Teacher Training and Parent Involvement

This intervention is led by a learning style expert(s), with all school personnel, including the principal, participating in the project. During the first trial after the training, the program is applied only to those students identified as having homework problems. After the program has been completed and evaluated, it can be extended with modifications to all students in the school. A policy decision on the scale of the intervention, however, should be made by the school administration before the project commences. The following program is one year in length and can be reduced for situations in which the entire school does not participate.

Step 1: Preparing for an Intervention—Teacher Training

Orientation

1. Begin with an awareness session to share the trainer's enthusiasm for training on home learning preferences.
2. Introduce theoretical and conceptual framework of the homework performance model.
3. Discuss the HMPQ and the profile with 21 components that HMPQ assesses (HMPP).
4. Spend time expanding knowledge and understanding of various theories and instruments of learning styles and the similarities

and differences between in-school and out-of-school learning styles or preferences (see chapter 3).

5. Have teachers become familiar with some of the research findings that support this approach for classroom and home applications.

Assess and Interpret the HMPQ

1. Administer the HMPQ to the teaching staff and interpret the results for them.

2. Discuss how they can incorporate the HMPQ assessment into their teaching repertoire.

Plan for Implementation

1. Develop a schoolwide system for implementing a homework motivation and preference program. For example, include HMPQ assessment into the comprehensive testing program; develop a student profile system for recording HMPP information about individual students; build a system for educating and informing parents; provide budgetary support for teachers to develop materials; establish an ongoing staff development program. In the first trial year, this step can be localized for the classrooms involved in the program.

2. Urge teachers to spend time discussing learning preferences with students. Students will come to see that differences in how people learn are normal and expected.

3. Have teachers administer the inventory to students.

4. Provide help for teachers in interpreting the results and planning homework strategies.

Step 2: Implementing the Program—Intervention

Identify Students with Homework Problems

1. Survey homework problems for all students using the modified Homework Problems Checklist (HPC; adapted from Anesko et al., 1987). Some of the HPC items on the homework situations are similar to those in HMPQ and are to be deleted.

2. Analyze the survey and find the students with homework problems.

3. Interview these students and find the reasons for homework problems. Pay attention to (a) their opinion concerning why they are having homework difficulties (e.g., boring, difficult); (b) when and how they usually do their homework; (c) when, how,

or under what conditions they do homework best when they do; and (d) the type of homework they like most or least.

Measure Their Actual Homework Style Using the HQ

1. Administer the HQ, an instrument assessing their perceived actual homework performance, to students identified as having homework difficulties.
2. Compare the results of the HMPQ and HQ by each component and find the discrepancies between them.

Parent Interview

1. Assess parental awareness of the child's homework motivation and preference. Administer HMPQ to parents, explain that the child completed the same scale, and ask parents to answer as if they are responding for their child.
2. Ask when and how their child usually does his or her homework, and ascertain whether there is any other environment in which homework can be done in the home.
3. Assess parental awareness of homework problems and what they have done to remedy the problems.
4. Explain that the parent and child HMPQ will be analyzed and findings will be recorded on the discrepancy between parental awareness of preferences and the child's strong preferences in doing homework. The homework strategy sheet containing the aforementioned information will be sent to the parent via the student in a few days. Additionally, telephone contacts will be made by the teacher.
5. Emphasize the need for teamwork by the student, teacher, and parent in this endeavor.

Analyses of Homework Questionnaire Responses

1. Analyze HMPQ/HQ of students and HMPQ of parents and determine the discrepancies.
2. Determine what teacher, parent, and student can do to facilitate students' homework motivation and preferences, based on these analyses.

Interview with Students

1. Discuss the HMPQ/HQ results of the students and parents.
2. Discuss what teacher, parent, student can do to help student do homework better.
3. Send the information to the parent via the student.

Communication with Parents (Telephone or Conference)

1. Confirm that parents received the letter.
2. Review the information with parents.
3. Discuss what parents can do to help and ask for cooperation at home. Teachers will be given helpful ideas on how to develop positive conversations with parents.

Intervention

1. Schedule regular student–teacher conferences, discuss whether the student is following the guidelines as given earlier, ask if the parents are supportive, contact the parents for continuing support and for discussing other homework-related questions.
2. Continue the teacher–parent intervention by accommodating the homework instructions and assignments and designing homework that allows students to use their strong perceptual modes.
3. Assess if the homework progress is being made. If there is no progress and the student has not improved in his or her attitude toward homework, consider supplemental efforts to meet the student's homework preferences (see chapter 8).
4. Continue to monitor the homework progress and to record observations on student's study habits, attitudes, and behavior changes.

Step 3: Postintervention

Administer Postintervention Measures

1. Administer student HMPQ/HQ.
2. Survey and interview to determine effectiveness of the intervention.
3. Review exam scores, homework scores (homework completion, quality, habit, attitude), and other relevant scores such as attitude toward school and classroom behavior.

Analyze, Discuss, and Report

1. Analyze postintervention measures.
2. Discuss results with students and parents.
3. Report findings to the principal for program evaluation.

Second Intervention: Parents as Homework Facilitators

This intervention program is designed for parents interested in taking an active role in contributing to a homework program for their child based on assessment of homework difficulty areas and of child's homework motivation and preference. This program is a modified version of a program implemented at the University of Utah Parent Homework Series (Jenson et al., 1995). The focus of this program, however, is on the promotion and accommodation by parents of their child's homework motivation and preference.

One major advantage in implementing the program involving parents is the relative ease of accommodating to individual differences. Adaptive instruction is problematic at school due to the large number of students manifesting various types of individual differences. By contrast, at home individual needs can indeed be accommodated. Although home learning should not be guided solely by the child's individual preferences, parents who have acquired the necessary knowledge can make informed decisions about how far they can and should go to help their child by accommodating to his or her preferences.

Major components of the Parents: Homework Facilitators program include the following:

1. Assessing areas of homework difficulties.
2. Assessing the child's homework motivation and preference using the HMPQ and actual homework performance using the HQ.
3. Assessing parental awareness of child's homework motivation and preference.
4. Analyzing the differences and similarities among these measured scores.
5. Establishing a channel of communication with the classroom teacher.
6. Implementing homework intervention.

This program consists of five sessions with approximately one- or two-week intervals between each session.

Session 1: Introduction and Assessment of Homework Difficulties

Introduction: Motivating Parents
1. Introduce the goals of the parent training and objectives of the current session.
2. Ask each parent to describe his or her child and the particular difficulties the child is having with homework. It is important for parents to see that other families have similar problems and that consistent effort on their part will improve their child's homework performance.

3. Summarize research findings about homework effects, both positive and negative; in-school and out-of-school learning preferences; the effects of accommodating learning preferences on student achievement and attitudes; and effects on student achievement of parental awareness of child's homework motivation and preferences. This summary provides additional motivation for parents, and addresses those situations in which only one parent values homework, while the other doubts its effectiveness.

Assessment of Student Homework Motivation Preference and Homework Problems

1. Introduce the measures used in the course of training—HMPQ and HPC (adapted from Anesko et al., 1987).

2. Inform parents that they and their child will be asked to complete these measures in order to determine parental awareness of child's homework behaviors.

3. Ask parents to bring the completed parent and child questionnaires to the next session for review. Caution them not to discuss the questionnaire while they are completing the items.

Session 2: Designing Homework Environment and Communicating with School Personnel

The session begins with an introduction of the objectives of the current session and proceeds with collecting the questionnaires distributed in the previous session. Session 2 should be held five to ten days following Session 1.

Gathering the Completed Questionnaires of Parents and Children

1. While the session continues with the next topic, training staff quickly analyze the responses, provide HMPP printouts highlighting each child's motivation source and strength and strong preferences, and the discrepancies between the child's and parent's responses.

Establishing Proper Communication Channel with Classroom Teacher

1. While the questionnaire responses are being analyzed, parents are given simple suggestions on good and poor communication techniques.

2. Parents also review different types of homework (practice, preparation, extension, and creative types) and how to judge good and poor homework assignments. (More on this topic is dis-

cussed in the next step with the interpretation of the HMPQ and HPC.)

Interpreting and Understanding the HMPQ and HPC

1. Provide parents with the printouts of their responses and give them ten minutes to reflect on the results. The trainer sits with parents who have questions about the results.

2. Instruct the whole group—conduct a discussion on the HMPQ and HPC results, focusing on parents' observations about the findings.

3. Encourage parents to bring a completed HMPQ and HPC to the first meeting with the teacher to discuss the homework preferences of their child and to point out specific areas of homework difficulties, especially those areas that teachers can make an effort to accommodate (e.g., modality preference, structure of homework instructions and assignments). Encourage parents to establish a special communication system (e.g., assignment checklist) for the child with the teacher to determine what homework was assigned, due dates, and whether homework was turned in.

4. Provide a few examples of a simple, one-page, daily assignment checklist and encourage parents to select or modify checklist and to discuss with the teacher whether he or she wants to modify it.

5. The classroom teacher is to initial the list of completed homework. It is the child's responsibility to fill in the name of the homework and to give the checklist to the teacher to be initialed.

Establishing Favorable Homework Environment

1. Have parents refer to the printouts of their child's HMPP and review its categories and components, focusing on their strong preferences and needs.

2. Discuss how to establish a supportive homework environment.

3. Provide guidelines for setting up a good home study area based on the HMPP information.

4. Emphasize that there is not a single environmental factor in isolation (e.g., sound or furniture) that a child prefers, but rather a combination of factors. For example, a child may prefer background music and a formal design of furniture.

5. Highlight the fact that parent's and child's preferences may be different and that parents should not force their preferences or views on their child.

Introduce the differences between "matching to the child's preferences" and "supplementing the child's preferences" and encourage parents to try the former first and the latter when necessary (see chapter 8). One may assume, for example, a structured, scheduled time that takes precedence over other activities (e.g., play, television, sports, special activities) is essential to completing homework (e.g., Jenson et al., 1995). However, when the child does not require a structured homework schedule, the parent might allow the child's preference to prevail and see whether his or her preferred way works. If not, the parent might supplement the child's preference with another method and monitor the progress. At this point, parents are provided with the research findings on the differences between the high- and low-achieving students on home learning preferences. This can be used as the primary source for supplementing the child's preferences.

Other workers in this field (e.g., Jenson et al., 1995) have provided their own set of rules for setting up the homework environment, and it is enlightening to compare their recommendations with those we offer: (a) Require that homework be done consistently in one place. Our view: Some students would prefer to change places for different subject matter. They might prefer to read on a couch, while working on math on the desk. (b) Limit others' access to the study area during homework time. Our view: Some students prefer to have authority figures (parents or older siblings) around when they do their homework. (c) Keep noise to a minimum during homework time. Our view: Noise level should probably be kept to a minimum; however, for those students who prefer to have background sound for the purpose of blocking other unnecessary thoughts, some music without lyrics should be provided. It has been found that Mozart scores enhance performance (e.g., Botwinick, 1997). Again, their preferred music can be tried first. (d) Make sure the work space is properly equipped (e.g., pencils, paper, erasers, etc.).

Discuss Things to Be Done

1. Instruct parents to discuss and set up a home environment with their child and to establish and main contact with the teacher.

Session 3: Motivating Students—Intrinsic and Extrinsic Motivation

This session meets five to ten days after Session 2. The session begins with a review of their activities since Session 2 (setting up homework environment and establishing contact with the teacher), a discussion of parents' observations. Session 3 is designed to provide parents with information on motivation research and to equip them with skills to motivate their child to complete homework.

Understanding Motivation

1. Review the motivational dimension of HMPQ: motivational source (self-, parent-, and teacher-motivated) and motivational strength (promptness and persistence), referring to the score on each component.

2. Review the literature on intrinsic and extrinsic motivation, discuss the pros and cons of the two types of motivation and the situations where each of the motivating philosophies and skills is appropriate (e.g., Chance, 1992, 1993; Kohn, 1993; Pintrich & Schunk, 1996; Stipek, 1993).

3. Provide various approaches to motivating students (e.g., use of incentives, kinds of incentives, and reinforcement schedules to increase desired behaviors). In many occasions, students with chronic homework problems will need a reinforcer or incentives to enhance motivation to do their homework until they reach the point where they are intrinsically motivated to do their homework for learning purposes.

4. Discuss and develop various incentives that might interest children instruct parents to discuss with their children possible incentives or rewards and to bring this information to the next meeting.

Session 4: Transferring Homework Guidance from the Parent to the Student

This session meets two weeks after Session 3. The session begins with reviewing parents' activities since Session 3 (setting up a motivation system—either extrinsic when deemed necessary or intrinsic). Parents present their system, focusing on their children's reaction to the idea of establishing the motivation system and their choice of rewards, and whether the motivation to complete homework is increased. Parents then make necessary adjustments of their motivation system.

Transferring Responsibility

1. Introduce the objectives of the current session. Parents want their children to be self-motivated and to assume responsibility for completing their homework. Parents who have used incentives for homework completion might be regarded by themselves and their children as controlling their children's behavior. In order for students to direct guide their own homework behavior, this parental control must be transferred to the student.

2. Provide self-monitoring techniques and materials for students to utilize. These include establishing and maintaining home environment for their homework, using a homework plan, completing homework assignment given daily. At first, self-monitoring can be aided by using planners, but with progress, use of a planner can be phased out. Students who self-manage homework think planners are not necessary and view them as a waste of time (Nelson et al., 1998).

3. Instruct parents to monitor the progress from time to time according to their scheduled contact time. They can phase out direct supervision by reducing the amount of contact with their children gradually as they progress on their own. Daily review of the assignment checklist can be reduced to twice a week, and then once a week. When parents think that their child does not need to be monitored by means of the assignment checklist, they can decide together to cease this practice, and have the child assume this responsibility. The parent can notify the teacher of this decision. However, noninvasive parental supervision is needed at all times in whatever form they chose to use.

4. Instruct parents to make notes on student progress and behavior change for Session 5.

Session 5: Post intervention

Parents will have had about three weeks to monitor the progress of their child's homework behavior by the time they meet for Session 5. The main purpose of this session is to share their experiences in the training program and to learn from other parents' experiences. By this time, some students will have established homework routines and self-control, whereas other parents are still providing homework guidance to their children. While sharing their experiences, parents can learn from other parents strategies that they have not yet tried.

Once parents conclude that homework completion is no longer a problem, the next step is to work on the homework quality. Students can monitor the quality of their work by using the homework quality checklist before they turn in homework and after the work is graded.

Parents should maintain contact with classroom teachers to inform them of the new steps they are trying, and to gain cooperation from the teacher. If the child refuses to do homework at this stage, parents and child should meet with the teacher and/or counselor to analyze the source of refusal, and treat the problems accordingly. For example, one of the reasons for students not completing homework is that the homework is inappropriate and/or irrelevant (Bacon, Chovelak, & Wanic, 1998). If this is a major source of the problem, parents may suggest that teachers modify the assignments to meet the individual student's needs.

In summary, the two homework intervention examples presented in this chapter are mainly based on our model of homework performance. The previous chapter also dealt with other important factors related to homework. These factors include exposure to various views on adaptive instruction, research findings on learning style interventions, and presentation of the complementary roles of parents, teachers, and students in solving homework problems. Chapters 9 and 10 discuss in more detail the helping strategies for each of the motivational and preference components.

9

Children's Structural and Motivational Needs in Homework

TEACHER STRATEGIES FOR HOMEWORK INSTRUCTIONS AND ASSIGNMENTS

Adapting Homework Instructions and Assignments

Teachers embracing the concept of home learning preferences should individualize homework instructions and assignments to accommodate individual differences in the way students prefer to study. All students will not do their homework equally well given the same homework instructions and assignments. For example, some students prefer to get detailed and exact instructions on how to prepare their homework and to be told exactly what they are required to do; others prefer to be free to exercise their own discretion and to handle their assignments in a flexible manner, and even to have some choice in the topic on which to work. Homework instruction should become as adaptive as classroom instruction. There is widespread acknowledgment that classroom instruction should be adapted for more effective teaching and learning (e.g., Burwell, 1991; McInerney, McInerney, & Marsh, 1997). The same should apply to homework instruction. Teachers should make available to their students several kinds of homework instructions along with various types of homework assignments to meet specific learners' needs. In doing so, teachers might well follow the general approaches described here. The structure component of the homework motivation and preference model is used as an example of an individualized approach, but other components of homework motivation and preference could just as easily be used.

Matching to the Student's Preferences

In this approach the teacher conducts a brief conference with the student to confirm the student's preference in homework instructions. If, for example, the student prefers unstructured homework instructions and assignments where he or she is given the opportunity to choose the kind of assignment, the pace, and/or other structural options, the teacher may concur with this arrangement for this particular student and for this particular homework assignment.

Because this approach considers a student's preferred mode of learning in designing and delivering homework, the homework completion rate and the quality of homework will presumably improve. Students will engage in homework preparation that requires less of a cognitive effort to adjust to the requirements. There is a reservation, however, that students' perceptions of their preferences may not be accurate or as effective for them as other study strategies may prove to be. Thus, for students whose preferences are not producing good homework, teachers may adopt a different approach, as described next.

Supplementing Student Preferences

When students' homework performance is deficient, does not improve by honoring their preferences, or both, teachers should introduce supplementary homework strategies and follow them up to see if they are more effective in improving homework achievement. Even when students do well with their primary preference (e.g., auditory), teachers may supplement their strong preference with another mode (e.g., providing homework assignments that require a visual or a kinesthetic mode of learning). Modification and extension of learning style can be effective when they take place in conjunction with changes that occur in student development (Davidman, 1981; Reid, 1987).

Research findings can be instructive in the choice of supplementary strategies. For instance, students who perceived their homework achievement to be of a high standard and expressed positive attitudes toward their homework tended to prefer structured homework instructions from their teachers, as compared with students characterized by low homework achievement (see chapter 5). This finding suggests that students with poor homework habits and negative attitudes toward homework might profit from more specific and detailed instructions on what they are required to do. Encouraging these students to acquire learning modes that were not originally part of their repertoire or preferences may help them do better in their homework and also in other learning situations. This expansion of the range of preferences and capabilities is also recommended for those who have positive attitudes and are doing well with their homework. Nevertheless, the students' preferred modes should be honored over the nonpreferred modes by the teacher as often as possible, especially when difficult homework is assigned.

As students become more aware of differences in their own learning preferences and in those of their fellow students (see chapter 7 for students' need for understanding their own learning preferences), they will appreciate the teachers' limited resources to accommodate each student's preferences in and out of class and instead of criticizing their teachers' teaching strategies, they will make better use of the resources that are available and recognize that expanding their preferred modes of learning is both an opportunity and a necessity.

Homework Design for Adaptive and Supplementary Approaches

An example of a general homework design approach that matches various types of homework content with home learning preferences is provided here.

(1) Perform a content analysis of homework and identify (a) purpose of homework; (b) type of homework (e.g., practice, preparation, extension/enrichment, creative); (c) type of resources required to do the homework (dictionary, library search, team work, community involvement); (d) learning preferences that can be accommodated, such as structured versus unstructured assignments and perceptual channels that can be used to do the particular homework (audiotapes, visual materials, hands-on materials, experiment, experiences).

(2) Create a chart for each homework purpose, with rows or columns for learning preferences/homework type; in each cell, provide resources needed to complete homework. Create various types of charts using the factors stated earlier.

(3) Identify those learners for whom a particular kind of homework assignment matches a particular set of student learning preferences.

(4) Teachers should identify those learners for whom they plan to supplement their preferences, by requiring them to use nonpreferred modes.

Other Effective Homework Practices

Other recommended homework practices are provided here (Patton, 1995):

(1) Establish a routine and schedule time for assigning, collecting, and evaluating homework. To make sure that assignments are understood by students, teachers must allocate sufficient time for explaining homework assignments. This is especially important for teachers who are im-

plementing the adaptive homework approach recommended here. When teachers explain the requirements and the choices in an organized manner, they are observed by the students who learn thereby how to organize their work (Epstein et al., 1993; Mercer & Mercer, 1993; Patton, 1995).

(2) Communicate to the students the consequences, both positive and negative, associated with homework performance. Academically responsible students will do their homework properly whether or not teachers establish and apply penalties for failure to complete assignments or to do them properly. However, most students do need to know the rules of the homework game, preferably from the beginning of the school year. Teachers might consider using a point system for various levels of completion and accuracy and include these points in the overall grade for the course. Daily notes about homework performance can be sent to parents for those students with homework problems (Patton, 1995; Patzelt, 1991; Polloway et al., 1995; Rosenberg, 1995).

(3) Present homework instructions clearly to students. If some students do not understand the instructions, they will do it incorrectly or they may fail to do it at all. If the teacher has prepared a chart of the content analysis, he or she would have the necessary homework information prepared for students. If rigorous individualization is required for a particular assignment, printed instructions should be prepared for each student. Extra time during or after class for additional explanation may be needed for students who have nonvisual learning styles. Even if the homework assignment, and especially the content, is the same for all students, different modes of presenting the instructions may exist.

(4) Make sure to clearly mention the due date and evaluation method for the particular assignment.

(5) Encourage students to ask questions about homework after instructions are presented.

(6) Involve parents in homework. Some parental involvement issues were previously discussed. When students are identified as having homework difficulties, the least their parents can do is sign the homework assignment when it is completed. Studies have shown a strong relationship between parents signing a completed assignment and the amount of time spent on the assignment by children (Holmes & Croll, 1989; Patton, 1995; Polloway et al., 1995).

(7) Evaluate the assignments. Although students do better homework when they know their work is being evaluated by their teachers, many teachers do not provide feedback on homework on a regular basis. Homework becomes more important and more meaningful to students when it is evaluated and used to determine a final grade. Given the limited amount of time at their disposal, homework evaluation has been a challenge to teachers. If teachers do not have the time to evaluate each student's homework, they need to reconsider the amount of homework they are assigning. There are some shortcuts. For example, structured

homework lends itself to scoring by teacher aides or by the students themselves using self-correction techniques or peer grading (Cooper, 1989b; Epstein et al., 1993; Frith, 1991; Mercer & Mercer, 1993; Patton, 1995; Pendergrass, 1985; Walberg et al., 1985).

ORGANIZING HOMEWORK AND THE HOMEWORK ENVIRONMENT

Most students have more than one homework assignment for the day. Some students like to decide on the order of the assignments before they begin working. They may assign order by a number of criteria: difficulty, the particular subject matter, or the due date. Others are less concerned about sequencing homework assignments, and plow through one assignment after another.

Students have preferences about the homework place: Some prefer to use the same place in the home on a regular basis, whereas others want to change places according to the subject matter or homework type, or just for the change. In a similar vein, some students like to do their homework at a set, scheduled time (right after school, in the evening, etc.), whereas others like to do it when they feel they are ready (e.g., when not tired).

Some organizational problems are the same for all students and their solution is the same. For example, teachers and parents must ensure that students have access to the books and other resource materials required to complete assignments. Teachers do this by providing information about where students will be able to access the materials (e.g., library search, Internet). Parents help their children with paper, pencils, calculators, dictionaries, books, and computers, making them available and keeping them within easy reach of the designated homework area. Students are more likely to use these materials if they are within easy access. For instance, if students do not have a dictionary close by, they are more likely to give up looking for the meaning of an unfamiliar word and simply glean its approximate meaning from the context in which it appears, thereby losing the opportunity to learn the exact meaning of a new word. (Consider how often we all do this.) Students also waste time locating these necessary supplies if they are not within reach. It is a common, but unfortunate, circumstance that the amount of time spent getting organized for homework takes up more time than the homework itself (Wood, 1987).

Structural Need

Students who prefer structured homework instructions and assignments want to receive detailed and exact instructions on how to prepare their homework. They want to know where they can go to receive help or find resource materials and when the homework is due. For these students, teachers should provide precise step-by-step instructions for each assignment with clearly stated homework purposes. It is useful to have these students work with an assignment notebook, to check in advance that they understand requirements and the sequence of tasks to be performed in completing the assignment, and to permit them to begin the assignment in class.

Students with homework difficulties are helped when an assignment with highly structured, sequenced content is broken down into smaller sections and students complete the assignment section by section. This highly structured approach, with follow-up section by section, will enable many students to acquire autonomous structuring skills for future assignments.

Capable students who prefer assignments with little or no structure welcome the opportunity to create something on their own, and most likely have their own ways of choosing what, when, and how they do their homework. Teachers should permit these students greater latitude than they permit less capable students in choosing topics, resources, procedures, time lines, and reporting approaches. Teachers may elect to set up a contract that specifies general guidelines for students, but contains choices in some categories.

Although there is a wide range of preferences, there are a few generalizations. First, more students prefer student-centered assignments over teacher-directed ones. Second, homework return rates are higher with student-centered homework than with teacher-directed work (Kogan & Rueda, 1997). Third, more motivated students (see chapters 3, 4, and 5) prefer structured homework. Fourth, most authorities on homework recommend that teachers provide structure and specific guidelines, but that they take into consideration students' age, ability, or achievement levels, and their individual preference for the degree of structure in homework.

Set Order versus Variable Order

This element is highly related to structure. Students who prefer structured homework tend to organize their assignments according to a certain order (e.g., from easy to hard assignments). This strategy is preferable for many reasons. It provides the advantages of self-pacing and the alternation of difficult and easy assignments, as well as allowing students to work according to subjective and objective priorities. Students should decide which subject to complete first by considering due dates, length, and difficulty of homework, and then order the remaining assignments accordingly to the same criteria. Parents of children who show an initial preference for organization can help their children achieve this approach. As children establish the order in which they will tackle various assignments, it is important that the required materials be available.

Organization-inducing tools are highly recommended for these students. A teacher-issued homework assignment notebook serves as a visual reminder of homework assignments to be completed. In and of itself, the notebook creates the opportunity to practice and perfect organizational and self-monitoring skills, and also encourages students to complete homework on schedule. Student portfolios or folders are also useful for organizing subject matter for schoolwork and homework assignments (Anliker et al., 1997; Bryan & Sullivan-Burstein, 1997). As students become used to one of these methods, they become self-directed learners who automatically use organizational skills. One of the most common characteristics of students with attention deficit hyperactivity disorder is their poor organizational abilities (Barkley, 1990; Stormont-Spurgin, 1997; Zentall, Harper, & Stormont-Spurgin, 1993). These students need continuing interventions to improve their organizational skills.

Set Place versus Variable Place

Some students prefer to do their homework in the same place in the house, whereas others prefer to use a variety of places. Some students even change places according to homework content; for example, when they are reading, they may use the living or family room where there may be an easy chair or a sofa. Other students change places for no specific reason, simply preferring to change places and have different objects around them. Still others change places because they do not have a specific place for homework or because there cannot be one in a small family residence; some may use the kitchen table after dinner.

If a student changes places out of choice and at the same time does homework poorly, parents may encourage the student to designate a specific place to study or provide a space for study. When considering a home learning environment, parents and students should also consider the other environmental factors discussed in chapter 10 in the section on surroundings.

Set Time versus Variable Time

When (time of day) students learn best varies from student to student. Unfortunately, students may not be able to choose to do their homework at the best time because it must be done after school (not their finest hours) or because they wish to engage in other out-of-school activities at that time. Some students are morning or early afternoon people and are most alert during school hours. When possible, students should be encouraged to do their homework when they are at their peak of alertness. This kind of timing is especially important in doing difficult assignments. Some students have no difficulty doing their homework at a uniformly high standard at different times of the day and require no special arrangements in this regard. However, students who do not schedule time for homework may be at risk of not completing homework because they may find valid reasons and invalid excuses to avoid doing their homework until the last minute. Setting a time establishes priorities among the many commitments of students and guarantees that the work will get done.

Scheduling when to do homework is problematic for students involved in many after-school activities. A weekly planner offers several advantages. First, it helps students schedule blocks of time for homework assignments and for schoolwork, a one- or-two-hour block of time each day when they can do their daily assignments. Second, it makes it easier for students to determine the amount of time required for long-term projects or to prepare for tests that may require a great deal of time for proper preparation. Third, the weekly plan encourages students to study daily and thereby reduces the probability of doing the homework at the last minute or cramming for tests. Fourth, it enables students to acquire time management skills, one of the most important study skills for students to acquire. Better time management affords students more time for study, other out-of-school activities, and even for resting and reflecting; poor time management is a frivolous waste of valuable time.

HOMEWORK MOTIVATION

One of the many potential benefits of homework is in fostering responsibility and independence (Cooper & Nye, 1994). Students who are motivated to do well on homework demonstrate self-discipline, self-direction, and independence in doing homework as well as in doing nonacademic activities. Self-motivated students are prompt and persistent in doing their homework, but not to the exclusion of motivation from parents or teachers. A strong preference for one source of motivation (e.g., self-motivation) does not exclude a substantial preference for a second source (e.g., teacher- or parent-motivated).

All students benefit from frequent reinforcements for working hard and doing well both in their schoolwork and their homework. Students who do their homework well so their parents or teachers will be proud of them need to receive demonstration of this pride. Some students make special efforts to get their parents or occasionally their teachers interested in what they are doing; others are self-motivated and do not need these evidences of adult approval (Hong, Tomoff et al., 2000).

Promoting Self-Motivation in Homework

Students' poor motivation to complete homework may be due to a combination of poor study skills, the absence of any interest, evaluation, or encouragement from teachers or parents, and the competition for the student's time of nonacademic activities (e.g., social events, hobbies, sporting events, or television) (Salend & Schliff, 1989a; Trammel et al., 1995). If they are able to acquire better study skills, they do better in school, become more motivated and have more positive attitudes toward school, in general, and homework, in particular. Thus, all of the variables associated with homework—learning preference, motivation, attitude, quality of homework performance, overall academic success—are related to one another; however, no single set of preferences guarantees success. Not all highly self-motivated students prefer unstructured homework, hence, the importance of cooperation between teachers and parents in accommodating to rather than working against children's learning preferences.

Students who are not motivated to do their homework tend to have low levels of content knowledge and basic study skills. Teachers need to consider these factors when planning homework (Epstein et al., 1993; Patton, 1995; Rosenberg, 1995; Salend & Schliff, 1989b). Repeated experiences of failure to complete homework have a cumulative negative effect on these students' self-esteem as learners and on their attitudes toward school. Teachers may decide to provide shorter and simpler assignments that can be completed with their current skills and to provide supervision and assistance so that these assignments are successfully completed. These students might also benefit from receiving incentives for completing their homework. Monitoring their own progress by keeping records of homework completion (e.g., self-recording and self-graphing) and by rating the quality of their work enable these students to become more self-reliant and to rely less on adult supervision (Dunlap, Dunlap, Koegel, & Koegel, 1991; Trammel et al., 1995). When extrinsic reinforcements (other than teachers' feedback on homework) are used to increase homework completion, they should be regarded as temporary and the reinforcement schedule should be adjusted so as to eliminate them entirely when students are intrinsically motivated to do their homework. For example, when students who used to hand in incomplete homework assignments start to submit complete ones, they are to be rewarded immediately and regularly until the new behavior becomes routine, and then rewarded intermittently, and eventually not at all, because the students have become self-motivated learners.

Parent-Motivated Students

Educators view homework as a way of including parents in the education of their children. Parents also see homework as a way, sometimes
the only way, to be included in their child's school life. It allows parents
to appreciate and support the work their children do. However, parental
involvement in homework can be negative if parents pressure children
or are confused about how to help them (Baumgartner, Bryan, Donahue,
& Nelson, 1993). As indicated previously, children appreciate their parents' interest and believe they do better in school with parental help;
however, they also have mixed perceptions on how much their parents
facilitate or confuse them when doing their homework (Balli, 1998; Cai,
Moyer, & Wang, 1997; Epstein, 1990; Finn, 1998). In general, there is a
positive relationship between parental involvement in homework and
student achievement and attitudes toward homework and school (Epstein, 1983, 1985; Hong & Lee, 1999a; Hong, Milgram, & Perkins, 1995;
Snow, Barnes, Chandler, Goodman, & Hemphill, 1991; Walberg et al.,
1985).

Those students who are strongly motivated by a parent benefit from
parental involvement. For example, parents may arrange for their child
to work on the assignments while physically near them. Some students
want their parents to watch them as they do their homework confidently
by themselves. Parents can set reasonable homework goals together with
their child, provide the circumstances that match the child's learning
preferences, provide the necessary resources, monitor the allocation of
time so there are no interruptions, assist in completing the homework,
provide enrichment activities, sign the completed work, and praise their
child for studious efforts and good work. Teachers can encourage positive parental involvement by sending notes home about some specific
assignments. Parents can use this information to acknowledge and show
interest in their child's schoolwork. Teachers may also praise children in
front of their parents at parent–teacher meetings.

Students who are not especially motivated by a parental figure should
be allowed to work alone, unless the child requests help. Many of these
students try to do their homework on their own, neither requiring nor
welcoming assistance or input from their parents. These children have
their learning preferences, however, and parents should be aware and
accommodating. Students need a library card and access to the nearest
public library. They may need their parents' help in obtaining the card
and in getting to the library. Whether the parent must be physically
present in the library to assist the child depends on the child's age and
capacity to use the library alone.

Teacher-Motivated Students

Teacher interest and reinforcement (praise, reward) can be very effective in promoting homework performance for students who are highly teacher-motivated. Most people appreciate hearing good things about themselves and students are no exception. Most students respond positively to teachers showing an interest in them and praising their good behavior, but teachers with large classes may not be able to attend appropriately to all of their students. It is especially important to identify those children who require a great deal of attention and reinforcement. Experienced teachers may be able to identify these students by observing their behavior, but may also rely on an assessment instrument such as the HMPQ.

Teachers must be tactful about the manner in which they show interest, give praise, or other rewards to students in public. Some students, even those who are teacher-motivated, are uncomfortable when they receive attention or praise in public (mostly older students). Praise can be given for any of the following: a specific accomplishment, completion of a difficult assignment or special project, showing improvement in one's work, trying to improve in one's work. For some students, trying to improve merits reinforcement, whereas for others, only higher levels of accomplishment are to be rewarded.

Teachers should be careful not to reward undesirable homework behaviors (e.g., handing in sloppy homework), nor be sarcastic about such behaviors. Constant attention from the teacher for undesirable behavior may well increase the likelihood of more undesirable behavior on the part of the student. Thus, if the teacher pays too much attention to inappropriate behaviors, it would be as if the teacher is encouraging the student to hand in sloppy homework, although the teacher really desires the opposite. Attention must be given, of course, to undesirable behavior that may be injurious or disruptive.

Students with homework difficulties benefit from additional teacher assistance, frequent monitoring by the teacher about the homework assignments, positive and reasonable expectations of success, taking effort into consideration in evaluation of a homework assignment, providing opportunities for extra credit, giving credit for homework completion in grading, providing corrective feedback, and positive, oral or written comments.

Teacher-motivated students will benefit from feeling treated as special, no matter to what the "specialness" refers. For example, in a study by Strukoff, McLaughlin, and Bialozor (1987, cited in Cooper & Nye, 1994), a daily report card system for homework was successfully used for certain children. When other students in the class expressed a desire also to have daily report cards, it became unclear whether the positive changes in homework behavior were due to the report card itself or to being singled out and receiving something "special."

Some students may be reluctant to acknowledge their desire for special attention from their teachers because of social opprobrium or because of their fears that others will confirm their worst fears about themselves, that they are "stupid." If they can be helped to achieve modest academic gains by a less direct approach, they will become sufficiently confident to accept greater involvement by their teachers and their parents. One way to help an academically weak and insecure student to make initial gains is to enlist peers, or preferably students somewhat older than the child, to serve as teacher aides with homework. If students prefer working with peers to begin with, this should be encouraged and made possible.

Homework Promptness and Procrastination and Persistence

Some students do not begin their homework until specifically reminded to do so. In general, it is not sufficient for teachers or parents to remind them of the homework; it also may be necessary to review with them what they have to do, how much time it is likely to take, and to indicate that their work is progressing (assuming that it is). One of the major reasons for procrastination or apparently forgetting to do an assignment is fear of failure or apprehension about doing something poorly. One way to deal with this apprehension indirectly is to review with the student what needs to be done, the amount of time that will be required, the help that is available if the assignment appears difficult, and to provide this help with ample encouragement.

Other students, especially older ones, may be resentful when adults remind them of homework assignments, expressing that they are willing to be held responsible for remembering homework assignments. It may be that they are already independent and responsible or that they are struggling to achieve independence and strive to complete homework without adult supervision and assistance (Retish, Hitchings, Horvath, & Schmalle, 1991). With these efforts to take responsibility for their work and to finish homework without procrastination, they will, in due time, acquire confidence in their ability to complete homework as well as other tasks and become independent and self-regulated learners (Warton, 1997).

For students who need to be reminded about homework, a daily and weekly homework planner can be used. Earlier examples used in helping students build organizational skills can also be used for helping student complete homework on schedule. For example, a homework assignment notebook or a weekly planner with places indicating blocks of time for each day where students can write their homework assignments and other activities can be used for the daily reminder as well as for the managing time for the week's various activities.

Encouraging students to set their own goals for homework completion would be another way to help avoid homework procrastination. A goal for one child might be to complete homework within one hour each day; a goal for another might be to complete a project by the following Saturday. Goals should be reasonable so that they can be accomplished. Miller and Kelley (1994) investigated the effects of goal-setting, which consisted of comparing performance goals against present performance level. This approach could also be viewed as a form of self-monitoring, in which children evaluate their own performance (Bandura, 1977, 1993). This strategy helped reduce children's homework difficulties with half of the participants showing on-task homework behavior.

With increasing homework responsibility and confidence, students benefit not only from being able to direct their own learning activities, but also from knowing how to seek assistance when needed. Students may ask teachers for clarification on homework instructions when they do not understand or are confused, contact library personnel, and use a homework hotline, if available, to get support (Patton, 1995). In any event, parents should not do the homework for their children. Even if parents often do this for various reasons (e.g., "Other parents do, so my child's grade will be influenced by those adult-helped projects"), doing homework entirely for children will impair rather than promote student responsibility.

Some students are persistent in homework completion, even when they face difficulties as they do homework. These students keep working until they solve problems and always finish homework. Most of these students start doing homework and prefer to finish one homework assignment before they start a new one. They need little supervision; however, if the student is also parent- or teacher-motivated, praise from them at the completion of the homework would further encourage and promote their persistent homework behavior.

For students with low persistence, using short-term assignments with interim due dates, reinforcing during the progress of completing homework, and providing periodic breaks would help them complete homework (Jonassen & Grabowski, 1993). These students also likely lack organizational skills; thus, an assignment notebook would help set the homework assignments in order, so they finish one homework after another, instead of putting aside the one that they were working on and start another.

Although we attempted to illustrate examples and strategies for each component of homework motivation and preference, teachers and parents should examine the student's motivation and preference in their entirety to properly prescribe strategies needed for helping students in homework completion.

10

Arranging Home Environment

This chapter discusses how parents can help design a home learning environment that matches or supplements their children's learning preferences.

DESIGNING HOME SURROUNDINGS

Dunn and Dunn (1992, 1993) indicated that the secret of designing an effective instructional environment in classrooms at little or no cost is using what is already there, but in new patterns. This concept also applies to designing learning environments in the home. An appropriate study area in the home is very important in order for the child to successfully do homework. When students are comfortable in their study environment, they are likely to have a better attitude about their homework, thus doing it better.

A walk through the hall of instructors' offices in a university might reveal that some instructors talk with students almost in the dark with all blinds shut, or with blinds wide open to get natural light from the outside. Other instructors work with lamps providing intensive spots of light, and still others work in a room that is entirely brightly lit. There is usually the faint sound of music coming from one or two of the offices. One instructor might bring in a small portable electrical heater because the room is too cold, while her neighbor is just fine with the room temperature. These examples of adult preferences in work environment confirm that individual differences in learning preferences are not confined to the developmental years, but are the rule for adults as well.

Children and adults both have learning preferences, but there are differences. Children are less likely than adults to be aware of their preferences and are also less able to modify their environment to their preferences. As students approach adulthood, however, they begin to "take care of themselves" and no longer need the cooperation of others (Hong, Tomoff et al., 2000). But before that time, they need the understanding and the cooperation of their parents in order to enjoy an optimal home learning environment.

Home environments vary a great deal. Some students have their own bedrooms, whereas others share a bedroom with one or more siblings. Some homes have study areas for family members to use, whereas others do not. There are formal desks and chairs for study in some homes, but not in others. If the home is relatively small and space is a premium, parents must be creative in utilizing the existing space and furniture to accommodate their children's homework preferences. The following general procedures are recommended in designing the homework environment:

1. The child should be involved in redesigning the space so that his or her needs and desires can be incorporated in the plan.

2. Possible changes should be discussed with the child before hand. The kind of involvement and discussion depend on the child's age and maturity. If the child is mature enough to plan by him- or herself, permit the child to do so and later to share the design plan.

3. After the home environment is rearranged, determine whether the new arrangement improves the child's attitude toward homework and the quality of the homework itself.

4. If the rearrangement does not appear to help, go back to the drawing board. Reevaluate the child's preferences and try to supplement them with other design approaches that have shown to be related to high homework achievement and positive attitude (e.g., high homework achievers on average prefer a quiet, well-lit environment with formal study furniture).

5. If the second arrangement does not work, consider whether the child's content knowledge, basic academic abilities, and study skills are commensurate with the requirements of the homework assignments. It is imperative to consult with the teacher and guidance counselor and to cooperate with them if a remedial

program is recommended. Modifications in the homework assignments may be necessary.

Suggestions for redesigning home surroundings are provided under
each category of background sound, light, temperature, and furniture
design.

Background Sound

Many students require a quiet environment when concentrating on
difficult material, others learn better with background sound than without (e.g., Pizzo, Dunn, & Dunn, 1990). For the latter students, sound
appears to block out other distractions. Music without lyrics seems to be
more conducive to learning than music with words because of the potential distraction of the lyrics (DeGregoris, 1986). Students who prefer
quiet need an area for homework that is free of television, radio, stereo,
household sounds, or street noise. The kitchen may be an acceptable
place to study after dinner, but an inappropriate place to study in the
afternoon hours because of the noise and activity in the room. If a noise-
free area is not possible, the child can use earplugs to block out the noise.

Some parents try to prevent their children from listening to music
while studying because of the assumption that it distracts, interferes, or
simply is enjoyable, whereas studying is a serious business. Nevertheless,
some children prefer background sound, whether classical or modern
music, while studying and may do better because of it. If parents find
that the child's music interferes with their own activities, the child may
listen to preferred music with earphones.

The way students combine homework and sound background depends on the type of homework and type of background medium (audio
media or TV). Students, in general, distinguish between cognitively complex assignments that tax their complete concentration and assignments
that are more routine and simple. Their performance on the former type
of assignment was impaired by the use of background media on the
average, whereas performance on the latter type of assignments was
somewhat increased by the use of background audio media (Beentjes,
Koolstra, & van der Boort, 1996). The frequency with which students in
Grades 5 to 8 used background sound was found to depend on subject
matter. Assignments combining reading and writing, writing only, and
mathematics were frequently combined with background sound,
whereas reading-only assignments were carried out without sound.
Background TV was found to interfere with performing difficult cognitive tasks, probably because attending to the assignment and to a television drama or comedy exceeds the attention capacity of most people

(Armstrong, 1993; Armstrong, Boiarsky & Mares, 1991; Armstrong & Greenberg, 1990).

Light

Most children appear to work well with normal variations in light. Some students study better in brightly illuminated rooms, whereas others study better in somewhat dimmer light, and should be permitted to do so. Similarly, some prefer overhead light that illuminates the entire area, others prefer limited light from a lamp that illuminates only the study materials. Whatever the source, insufficient lighting will cause eye strain and fatigue. The desk or table in the study area should be positioned to provide for proper lighting. Students who prefer bright light may move the desk near the window and/or use lamps with stronger voltage, and the reverse for those who prefer a lower level of light. Parents and students may choose among various kinds of lamps (fluorescent, soft light, ceiling lamps, desk lamps, floor lamps). A direct lighting system, in which the light is directed downward, is recommended when students are required to read materials written in varied sizes of print and types of paper in a single homework session (Wood, 1987). On the other hand, fluorescent lighting may overstimulate some children and elicit hyperactivity and restlessness (Dunn, Krimsky, Murray, & Quinn, 1985). The background color of computer monitors can also be adjusted to reduce light intensity.

Temperature

Temperature variations affect individual students differently. Some students have high tolerance for variations in temperature even when it is above or below their preferred degree, whereas others only work well within a particular temperature range. Some students learn better in a warm room (because it keeps them comfortable), and others in a cool room (because it keeps them alert; Murrain, 1983). Extreme heat is a stressor that taxes the body and the mind and makes learning difficult both at school and at home; a warmer than normal temperature tends to make students work at a somewhat slower rate than usual. On the other hand, students lose interest in studying when the room temperature is excessively low (Wood, 1987). Parents should pay attention to children's temperature preferences, especially those of young children, and adjust the heating or cooling system accordingly. If a control system is not available, then putting on or removing clothing can help. The same applies to the use of a fan or a space heater.

Formal versus Informal Furniture Design

A desk, a kitchen table, or a folding table are all solutions to the child's need for a work surface. Study furniture is even more flexible. A bed, couch, easy chair, or even the floor can be a place where one reads. Some parents might think that informal seating arrangements distract students from the serious business of concentration. This blanket judgment is as often incorrect as it is correct, and it may depend on the assignment as much as on the child. Some children need to feel comfortable and relaxed before they begin to study, and learn better with informal seating arrangements than with the typical student desk and chair. The students' furniture preferences may also depend on the homework content, reading for understanding without note taking versus math calculation. The former can be done almost anywhere, the latter requires a writing surface and possibly access to a calculator or a computer.

Some of these preferences are highly subjective and idiosyncratic. For example, some students like clutter on their work surface, whereas most students find it distracting and disruptive and prefer a study surface, whether desk or kitchen table, that is free of unnecessary objects. Some children prefer a formal study environment (chair, desk) and enter into this distinct setting with confidence. Research has shown that high achievers prefer a formal design. By contrast, others are apprehensive about schoolwork in general and prefer an informal environment that more closely approximates nonacademic recreational activities with which they are comfortable. If a child prefers an informal design but is not performing well on school or homework, it may be advisable to shift to a desk and chair and to deal with the causes of the apprehension. Some preferences are invariant. If children elect to study while sitting on a chair, or if they require a comfortable writing surface, the height of the chair must be appropriate and comfortable; an uncomfortable and unadjusted chair causes fatigue and even pain in the legs or back.

SMALL-GROUP HOMEWORK

Although some students prefer to study alone, other students learn best when they study with their peers. They do so for any number of the following reasons:

1. The interaction of friends stimulates them to learn.

2. Sharing responsibility for the assignment with others enables them to work in a more relaxed manner.

3. They can deal more effectively with a specific portion of an assignment rather than with the entire task.

4. They can learn from their peers.

5. A larger commitment is felt to their peers than to their parents, teachers, or even to themselves (Dunn & Dunn, 1992, 1993).

Research has indicated that matching opportunity with preferences for learning alone or learning with peers is more effective than a non-matched coercive approach (Dunn, Ginnitti, Murray, Rossi, & Quinn, 1990; Miles, 1987; Perrin, 1984). Parents' notions of what is best for their child on this matter, as on others, is counterproductive, and parents are encouraged to be open-minded, and to consider the child's wishes. When parents listen to their children and make decisions and corresponding arrangements conducive to better homework done alone or in groups, children perceive their parents in a more favorable light, as interested and supportive of their work in and out of school. Research also tends to confirm that older children study together more often than their younger counterparts. For example, more seventh graders than fifth graders preferred to study with peers (Hong & Lee, 1999a), and junior high students are more likely than elementary students to report that a friend helped them with homework (Bryan & Nelson, 1994).

There are many psychological and behavioral gains in doing homework with others, but there are also adverse effects. Some students come to depend on their peers heavily and are unable to work alone; some take advantage of the group and become free-riders. As a consequence, more capable students may come to resent working in a group because the work is not shared equally and free loaders get the credit for their work. Some prefer to work independently to begin with because they have the knowledge, skills, and self-confidence to complete homework independently. It is thus not surprising to see that high achievers prefer to do their homework alone (Hong, 1998; Hong & Lee, 1999b).

Teachers are in a position to encourage the formation of homework groups among those students who show this preference on the HMPP. They may do so by designing homework projects that require collaboration in pairs or in teams of three or more. Students who prefer to work independently should be given the opportunity to do so. Nevertheless, teachers may deliberately involve these students in group projects in order to encourage the development of their social skills and the tolerance necessary for successful group collaboration in the future.

Homework may be designed for groups of varying sizes and purposes:

1. A group constituted to help one another with homework is an obvious option.

2. A group of students may study together as a team for a competition in which the team with the highest average score of its members wins.

3. A group may be assigned the task of brainstorming on a particular topic, with group members producing more ideas than individual members working alone.

Teachers should show students some of the useful techniques that enhance performance in groups: how to work together, how to correct each other's work, how to quiz each other, and how to say nice things to each other. Groupwide assignments also can be done on school grounds or outside the school. The purposes and ground rules for group formation must be carefully thought through by teachers before they approach the students; otherwise, students will become confused and upset if not chosen to participate in certain groups. Group study (e.g., a three-member team) was recommended for students who are average or below average in mathematics because of the benefit they derive from cooperative learning. High math achievers prefer to work alone, although they continue to excel when they work in groups (Ma, 1996). More research is needed to find favorable group sizes for other homework contents.

Most parents are used to their children doing homework assignments on their own. They are not accustomed to the group homework projects that require hosting their children's classmates in their home or having their children go to someone else's home to do homework. They may raise a legitimate concern that their children will spend more time socializing than studying. When teachers initiate group homework projects, they have a responsibility to explain the rationale and the ground rules to the parents, especially if these projects are specifically designed for their own children.

The initiative for group homework may come from the children themselves and the parents may turn to the teachers for guidance as to how to proceed. In general, parents should allow child-initiated group homework to take place if certain conditions, such as those that follow, are spelled out in advance by the parents and are met by the children:

1. Parents must monitor the work product to ensure the homework is completed.

2. The quality of the homework is maintained at a high level, and if originally low, it must be raised by group homework.

3. The host parents as well as the parents of the other children must be comfortable with the arrangement.

4. If the conditions are not met, the arrangement will be discontinued not as punishment, but simply as evidence that it is not working.

5. Group homework should not be used as a substitute or an excuse for informal social gatherings of friends. Other opportunities for social gatherings devoid of any academic goal should be available for the children.

PARENTAL INVOLVEMENT OR INTRUSION: THE NEED FOR AUTHORITY FIGURES

L. P. Campbell (1997) urged educators to recognize that K–12 students desire their freedom, but must be given that freedom only in doses commensurate with maturity. Many students are in desperate need of authority figures to provide them with structure, directions, rules, and limits that they do not know how to provide for themselves. Students who in fact need adult supervision in their lives may express the diametrically opposite preference to be free of adult supervision. The latter is the socially desirable response for adolescents and many adolescents are more comfortable asserting their desire for independence than acknowledging their personal misgivings about being able to exert responsible control over their lives. This may be why some parents who received their child's HMPP chart found the child's preference for doing homework without the presence or supervision of an adult to be unacceptable and did not want to support this preference (Hong, Tomoff et al., 2000).

Parental involvement may be appropriate or excessive. It can become intrusive and counterproductive. Some parents do not allow their children to figure out problems on their own, and after a short pause give the solutions themselves. Other parents confuse their children by showing them a "better" way, not realizing that current instructional methods are different from those used when they were in school. Parental insistence that children must complete their assignments to their satisfaction may not be helpful and may even be harmful to their relationship as well as to the goal of the assignment—that children do their homework with a positive attitude and in a proper way. Parents must remember that they assume an important role in homework when they provide a favorable homework environment and answer any questions their children may have, but they are not to do the homework for them. The way they treat their children during the homework process may alienate their children from them rather than bring them closer together. Parents must learn to be patient and to respond to their children's questions in a way that does not discourage or disparage them. When parents command or threaten, they are not being helpful. Instead they should learn to focus on positive aspects of their children's homework and offer encouragement and praise at the right time.

Many parents trust their children to behave in a responsible manner both in school and when doing homework. Trust comes easy when children are good students. One parent mentioned that her child does her homework in another section of the house where no adults can observe. The mother is comfortable with this arrangement, even though it is different than the way she herself did homework (Hong, Tomoff et al., 2000).

Children's preference for the presence of an authority figure while doing homework should be considered, even if the student is a high achiever. Some students do better when they have an adult figure around (e.g., parent, older sibling, grandparent, guardian). Students who do well see themselves as behaving responsibly and as not being in need of adult presence or supervision. Students who do poorly may perceive adult presence as an additional source of pressure and as evidence that they are incapable of handling school assignments on their own. Research suggests that those children who objectively need help appear to receive it from their parents. Students in special education are more likely than students in regular education to have adults, chiefly parents, help them. Similarly, younger students are more likely than older peers to receive help from parents with their homework (Bryan & Nelson, 1994).

Students who prefer to have an adult around perceive parental presence and involvement as evidence of interest and support. These students appreciate their parents checking their completed work. If parents see that their children are having difficulties doing homework, they may try to understand why, record the relevant behaviors of their children, and share this information with the teachers. This insight and information may point to the source of the child's difficulties. The child may not be paying attention at school when the homework is being given out, the assignment may be too difficult or too long, or there may be too many distractions at home. Parental input may help develop a strategy for solving the problem cooperatively (Doyle & Barber, 1990). Home–school communication can be further facilitated with a homework assignment notebook or planner in which parents and teachers can check for homework completion and have space for writing their observations on the child's homework behavior.

DESIGNING HOMEWORK TO ACCOMMODATE CHILDREN'S PERCEPTUAL STRENGTHS

The research on the match of perceived perceptual modality of the learner and the required perceptual modality of the material to be mastered in the classroom is conclusive. Dunn, Beaudry, and Klavas (1989) and Dunn and Dunn (1992, 1993) summarized the studies on the effects of matching classroom instructional strategies and materials to children's perceptual strengths on academic performance. When students are introduced to new or difficult materials through their preferred perceptual modes (auditory, visual, tactile, or kinesthetic), they remember and learn more than when they are introduced to this material through their least preferred modality (e.g., Bauer, 1987; Ingham, 1989; Martini, 1986; Riding & Burt, 1982). The same is true of adults. When students in continuing adult education are taught by matching instructions to auditory, visual, and tactile perceptual preferences, significant positive gains in achievement are observed (Buell & Buell, 1987). It is reasonable to predict that students will benefit from a corresponding match of preferred modality and learning requirements outside the classroom, in homework.

When students are taught through a nonpreferred perceptual modality, they may still learn, but may gain and understand less than if their preferred modality is accommodated. Children in some cultures learn by observing (visual), imitating, and experiencing (tactile and kinesthetic). Children in modern classrooms mostly learn by listening (auditory) to teachers and reading (verbal–visual) what is on the board or in the books and notes. This educational practice matches those students with auditory and visual preferences and they have less problems absorbing and retaining new or difficult materials, than children who prefer to learn by doing and sensing through their body sensation or movement (touching and manipulating materials or participating in real-life activities). These latter children are at a decided disadvantage in dealing with auditory–verbal–visual materials.

Some students have said that it is easier to learn by reading and analyzing figures in their head than to learn by means of manipulating objects. This is especially true of older learners because people tend to become more verbal, and visual, tactile, and kinesthetic skills become less important as they get older (James & Galbraith, 1984; Lowenfeld, 1987). Students gradually learn to adapt their nonmatching modalities to deal with the demands of the learning environment (Hong & Suh, 1995; Reid, 1987), but in the process of adapting, they may be losing the opportunity to fully develop their learning potentials. This can be a serious problem for students who start off with learning difficulties.

Teachers can accommodate students' preferred perceptual modalities when designing homework assignments. Most homework assignments consist of reading, writing, or both, but assignments can include going places, gathering things, interviewing people, building things using materials existing at home, and doing other creative projects. Some students like hands-on homework that requires creativity and dislike boring, routine busywork (Hong, Topham et al., 2000). Homework sheets that explain hands-on science activities that utilize materials available in the home and require parental cooperation was found to increase students' positive attitudes about school science and parental involvement in homework activity (Rillero & Helgeson, 1995). These findings suggest that teachers should design homework stressing various modalities for at least a portion of homework assignments throughout the school year.

In providing homework instructions, teachers may use an overhead projector to accommodate both auditory and visual learners. An opportunity for manipulative activities or role-playing can be provided when presenting the assignment to students and when students present their completed assignment in class. Given limited resources and time, perceptual modes may not be easily arranged; nevertheless, teachers should strive to utilize various sensory channels, so that students can model their teachers and use their preferred modalities wherever possible in doing their homework.

A program using graphic organizers to enhance reading comprehension in content areas provided strong support for the inclusion of visual graphic materials in the classroom curriculum (Agnello, Jockl, Pearson, & Velasco, 1998). In this study, graphic visual–spatial materials (graphs, charts, diagrams, and pictures) were superior to visual–verbal materials in enhancing reading comprehension and in elevating positive attitudes toward reading both for students who preferred the visual–spatial channels and for students who did not. Dunn (1992) also encouraged teachers to use tactual and kinesthetic materials and activities for teaching word recognition.

Suggestions for instructional strategies that highlight particular perceptual modalities are summarized here (Dunn & Dunn, 1992, 1993; Jonassen & Grabowski, 1993). Some of the recommendations are self-evident, but merit mention, clarification, and comment.

(1) *Auditory* learners learn best from modes of communication that utilize sound, including lectures, tapes, and verbal explanations of written material. This means that teachers read aloud and explain to students having difficulty with their homework assignments. These students read aloud what is presented on the board or transparency. Before getting started on homework, they read aloud the homework directions to themselves or to their parents, or their parents to them.

(2) *Visual* learners are more likely to learn best from visual modes of communications and instructional materials, reading-oriented tasks, interpreting graphs, charts, diagrams, illustrations, or video. These materials are also appropriate for homework assignments. Strategies such as using mnemonics, visual memory supports, imaging, concept mapping, handouts, or underlining, are helpful, especially when assignments involve difficult materials.

(3) *Tactual* and *kinesthetic* students learn better from doing homework that requires learning through physical manipulation of materials such as creative hands-on tasks, learning mathematics by manipulating objects, tasks that require making, building, and actually experiencing, or gamelike homework assignments. Students may borrow the materials

used in class for homework and return them next morning. If this is not feasible, students are encouraged to duplicate or find similar materials at home for completing homework. Preparing hands-on learning materials can be the homework assignment itself. Teachers might assign groups with specific tasks that require manipulations. For example, making a set of flash cards for vocabulary learning or multiplication table, or building science set for a particular content. Providing opportunities for students to plan and attain real-life experience, such as visits, interviews, participating in grocery shopping for specific homework purposes, and other various projects, are good examples of learning through a kinesthetic channel. Dramatic presentation can be an effective form of kinesthetic homework. If, however, teachers do not use these approaches in their classrooms, it will be difficult for students to imagine and create them while doing homework.

(4) Students also need to learn through their nonprimary perceptual modality to complement or expand their repertoire of preferred modes of learning. Simultaneous presentations of learning materials and homework assignments using a multisensory approach (e.g., visual and oral presentations), providing or allowing auxiliary learning aids such as calculator or computer for homework completion, or allowing alternative response formats for homework presentation (e.g., oral rather than written), will help students expand their capabilities in the different modalities.

When the primary teaching mode is not effective for particular students, it should be supplemented with other approaches. For example, when verbal instructions for language or writing show little effect, physical movement or manipulatives that draw on spatial ability can help students understand language structures in nonverbal ways (Hecker, 1997; Price, 1995). A writing process program that facilitated visual, kinesthetic, and verbal modes of thinking in children was also successful (Olshansky, 1995). Efforts to require the use of nonpreferred as well as preferred modalities are very worthwhile and will enable students to become comfortable learning from materials using various perceptual channels.

Research findings on the efficacy of a particular instructional approach must be treated with caution. A recent study compared the effects of two teaching approaches, worksheets versus manipulative Algeblocks on achievement in mathematics, with other variables controlled (lecture and homework). The findings were higher achievement for the worksheet group (McClung, 1998). Unfortunately, individual differences on perceptual modality was not taken into consideration, and we do not know whether the students in the two groups were comparable in visual or tactile preferences in learning. Without this knowledge, it is difficult to conclude whether medium (manipulatives vs. worksheet) or the preferred perceptual modality had more influence on achievement differences in the two groups. Future studies may use the perceptual modality as an experimental or control variable in investigating instructional media effects.

ARRANGING OPPORTUNITY FOR INTAKE AND MOBILITY IN LEARNING AT HOME

Because background sound helps some students concentrate on homework, eating or chewing may have similar effects on other students (see chapter 1). Some students like to stay in one place for long periods of time to learn, whereas others need to move around in the room or in the house or even walk around while studying. Parents and children are frequently in conflict when their beliefs and practices on intake and mobility preferences do not agree. When children express their needs for food and mobility when doing homework, parents may disagree because of their views on what is best for student learning. Some parents try to convince or force their children to conform to their wishes. However, studies show that satisfying these bodily needs helps students learn better (e.g., Della-Valle et al., 1986; MacMurren, 1985; Miller, 1985).

When we were young students, occasionally my friends and I got together after school to do our homework. Parents, mostly mothers, usually came in the room quietly with a bowl of fruit and snack, saying "Have some food while you study" and disappeared quietly. I do not remember whether we immediately plunged into the food or not, but I often wonder whether these parents knew about our need for food intake, or was it just an advanced reward for doing a good job with our homework?

One thing that is reassuring about meeting students' bodily needs during homework time is that there is no need to worry about disturbing other students as might happen in classrooms. Parents should permit children to snack or drink or to move about while doing homework, if they wish to do so. Parents do have a responsibility to monitor what is going on when they permit these things, to determine if they facilitate or interfere with competing homework assignments in a proper fashion.

In summary, solving homework difficulties and inculcating good homework habits is a team approach that requires the cooperation of the teacher, the parent, and the student. Children's learning preferences are a part of the effort, the creativity, and tact of teachers and parents are another part. Careful follow-up of these efforts and the decision to try something else when the initial arrangements are not working is a third part.

Many books that deal with learning in school can be profitably used for enhancing learning out of school. These books originally designed as resources for preservice and in-service teachers to improve learning in classroom environments (e.g., Dunn & Dunn, 1992, 1993; Griss, 1998) are helpful for homework assignments as well. They provide valuable information for teachers and parents, but do not supplant the unique contribution of the present volume in maximizing the information provided by children's homework motivation and learning preferences to help them do better in their schoolwork in and out of the classroom.

These preferences are obtained by self-report and as such are vulnerable to distortion as well as to lack of clarity (Jonassen & Grabowski, 1993). Children and adults alike are not necessarily aware of their learning preferences accurately. They may accept existing conditions without realizing that under other circumstances they would find learning far more pleasurable, and far better understood and retained. This is why follow-up monitoring is essential when we implement a home learning preference approach to ascertain the success or failure of an apparent match or mismatch of preferences and learning circumstances.

Epilogue

THE THREE-WAY PARTNERSHIP

Homework is a cost-effective teaching tool if it is designed and managed well. This book emphasized the importance of the student–teacher–parent partnership in understanding, assessing, and applying students' homework motivation and preference in improving attitudes and homework achievement. Classroom teachers must recognize that they themselves not only learn differently, they also teach differently and that teaching strategies are not equally effective for all children. What may be an optimal teaching strategy for one student may impede another. Parents must become equally aware, otherwise they will be unable to recognize and respect the ways their children learn best, especially if children's preferences differ from those of the parents. Teachers and parents should collaborate to ensure that a variety of home learning opportunities are provided for children. Finally, students must shoulder their responsibilities by being aware of their own preferred ways of learning and studying. They must assert their preferences tactfully, but firmly. Once their preferences are addressed, they must take responsibility for their part of the teaching–learning process in and out of school, and do their best because they now have the opportunity to do so.

We began this book by introducing the conceptual and theoretical background of our homework performance: motivation and preference model, and by focusing on the similarities and differences of in-school and out-of-school learning preferences. We presented an instrument that assesses students' homework motivation and preference and traced its empirical development and validation history. We analyzed the similarities and differences between preferred and actual homework performance across various cultures and grade levels. We showed the effects on children's attitudes and achievements of parents' recognition of their children's homework motivation and preferences, and their inferred accommodation with these motivations and preferences. Differences in homework motivation and preference were found between high- and low-achieving students, along with evidence that matching children's preferred–actual homework preferences contributed to higher homework achievement. The homework motivation and preference of individuals who were gifted in various subject matters were reported.

Parent, teacher, and student roles in solving homework problems were discussed in the context that the three-way partnership is critical for homework success. Two homework intervention programs were presented that emphasized again the three-way partnership. Additionally, strategies that teachers and parents can employ to help students do their homework well were illustrated for each homework motivation and preference component. These efforts at homework individualization can only be effective, however, if school administrators support teachers' efforts in this direction by providing the necessary resources, as well as endorsement and praise for these efforts.

Two Caveats

Many of the chapters in this book focused on group differences in homework motivation and preference by country, age, gender, and achievement levels. It would be unfortunate if these group data diminished in any way the realization that every learner, adult or child, is unique in his or her homework motivation and preferences. Teachers need to recognize each student's unique needs and even more important to create conditions to satisfy them. Is this a challenge or an impossible mission? It is not impossible for the parents. It is far easier for parents, than for teachers dealing with many children, to recognize their children's unique needs and to find ways to satisfy them. The partnership of teachers and parents, however, will enable both to help each student learn better in school, and especially at home. What has been learned from research on the homework motivation and preference in different groups of learners enriches the understanding of the construct and leads us to devise more effective homework interventions for students, teachers, and parents.

There is another potential danger in the emphasis on homework motivation and preference. It might lead one to ignore many other equally important student abilities, including learning aptitudes, interests, and patterns of interpersonal relationships with parents, teachers, siblings, and peers. When teachers and parents customize children's homework assignments and their homework environment, they should follow up to ascertain whether customization is working. Parents may check that homework is completed. The teacher has the responsibility to monitor the quality of what is completed. If the interventions are not successful, teachers and parents should attempt to try something different, always keeping in mind that there are many variables other than motivation and preference that affect homework performance.

The Challenge of Technology

Advances in computer technology permit educators to incorporate the new concepts discussed in this book into course design and development and classroom instruction (Caudill, 1998; Fucaloro & Russikoff, 1998). These advances also permit us to ascertain whether new instructional methods modify or even magnify children's learning style. Some studies report change in learning style as a function of computer-assisted learning (e.g., Clariana, 1997), whereas others are inconclusive (e.g., V. Cohen, 1997). Another research topic has been to match various approaches in teaching via the Internet and other hypermedia with individual learning styles (e.g., Kerka, 1998).

As the Internet and other computer-based communication tools become prevalent in homes, students' use of these tools for their homework will rise. Researchers have already begun to examine the ways that families make use of computer technology for educational purposes (Fishman, Kupperman, & Soloway, 1998). Students have already been using the computer technology in completing their homework assignments, for example, by searching web sites and using CD-ROMS for research projects, communicating with peers and experts through the Internet, and using the computer as a tool for writing and graphing. A systematic use of computer technology for homework design offers other exciting possibilities for individualizing homework for students. The goal of a computer in every home is not yet realized, but teachers should recognize that computers can be the homework tool of choice for many learners and should use them in planning individualized homework assignments. Computer technology for homework was not a focal point in this volume. However, future books and articles on homework design and strategies will undoubtedly include the use of computer technology, as more empirical evidence on the instructional effectiveness of this technology accumulates.

References

Abbott-Shim, M. S. (1990). Inservice training: A means to quality care. *Young Children, 45* (2), 14–18.

Agnello, C., Jockl, P., Pearson, I., & Velasco, D. (1998). *Improving student reading comprehension in the content areas through the use of visual organizers.* Master's Action Research Project, Saint Xavier University and IRI/Skylight, IL. (ERIC Document Reproduction Service No. ED 420 853)

Alleman, J., Brophy, J. (1991). *Reconceptualizing homework as out-of-school learning opportunities.* East Lansing: Michigan State University, Institute for Research on Teaching.

Anderson, C., Bassett-Anderson, M. K., Gerretsen, D., & Robilotta, G. (1997). *Student responsibility in school and home environments.* Master's Action Research Project, Saint Xavier University and IRI/Skylight, IL. (ERIC Document Reproduction Service No. ED 412 015)

Anesko, K. M., & O'Leary, S. G. (1982). The effectiveness of brief parent training for the management of children's homework problems. *Child and Family Behavior Therapy, 4,* 179–185.

Anesko, K. M., Schoiock, G., Ramirez, R., & Levine, F. M. (1987). The Homework Problem Checklist: Assessing children's homework difficulties. *Behavioral Assessment, 9,* 179–185.

Anliker, R., Aydt, M., Kellams, M., & Rothlisberger, J. (1997). *Improving student achievement through encouragement of homework completion.* Master's Action Research Project, Saint Xavier University and IRI/Skylight, IL. (ERIC Document Reproduction Service No. ED 415 022)

Archer, A. L. (1988). Strategies for responding to information. *Teaching Exceptional Children, 20*(3), 55–57.

Armstrong, G. B. (1993). Cognitive interference from background TV: Structural effects on verbal and spatial processing. *Communication Studies, 44,* 56–70.

Armstrong, G. B., Boiarsky, G. A., & Mares, M. L. (1991). Background TV and reading performance. *Communication Monographs, 58,* 235–253.

Armstrong, G. B., & Greenberg, B. S. (1990). Background TV as an inhibitor of cognitive processing. *Human Communication Research, 16,* 355–386.

Bacon, L., Chovelak, C., & Wanic, A. (1998). *Instructional techniques to improve homework completion with sixth grade and Spanish I students.* Master's Action Research Project, Saint Xavier University and IRI/Skylight, IL. (ERIC Document Reproduction Service No. ED 4222 115)

Balli, S. J. (1998). When mom and dad help: Student reflections on parent involvement with homework. *Journal of Research and Development in Education, 31,* 142–146.

Bandura, A. (1977). *Social learning theory.* Englewood Cliffs, NJ: Prentice-Hall.

Bandura, A. (1993). Perceived self-efficacy in cognitive development and functioning. *Educational Psychologist, 28,* 117–148.

Barbe, W. B., & Milone, M. N., Jr. (1981). What we know about modality strengths. *Educational Leadership, 38,* 378–380.

Barkley, R. A. (1990). *Attention deficit hyperactivity disorder: A handbook for diagnosis and treatment.* New York: Guilford.

Barron, F., & Harrington, D. M. (1981). Creativity, intelligence and personality. *Annual Review of Psychology, 32,* 439–476.

Bauer, E. (1987). Learning style and the learning disabled: Experimentation with ninth graders. *Clearing House, 60,* 206–208.

Baumgartner, D., Bryan, T., Donahue, M., & Nelson, C. (1993). Thanks for asking: Parent comments about homework, tests, and grades. *Exceptionality, 4,* 177–183.

Beentjes, J. W. J., Koolstra, C. M., & van der Boort, T. H. A. (1996). Combining background media with doing homework: Incidence of background media use and perceived effects. *Communication Education, 45,* 59–72.

Biggs, J. (1979). Individual differences in study process and the quality of learning outcomes. *Higher Education, 18,* 384–394.

Blackfelner, C., & Ranallo, B. (1998). *Raising academic achievement through parent involvement.* Master's Action Research Project, Saint Xavier University and IRI/Skylight. (ERIC Document Reproduction Service No. ED 421 273)

Bloom, B. S. (1985). *Developing talent in young people.* New York: Ballantine Books.

Botwinick, J. (1997). *Developing musical/rhythmic intelligence to improve spelling skills.* Master's Action Project, Kean College of New Jersey. (ERIC Document Reproduction Service No. ED 405 548)

Boulmetis, J., & Sabula, A. M. (1996). Achievement gains via instruction that matches learning style perceptual preferences. *Journal of Continuing Higher Education, 44*(3), 15–24.

Bryan, T., & Nelson, C. (1994). Doing homework: Perspectives of elementary and junior high school students. *Journal of Learning Disabilities, 27,* 488–499.

Bryan, T., & Sullivan, K. (1995). *Teacher selected strategies for improving homework completion.* Unpublished manuscript, Arizona State University, Tuscon.

Bryan, T., & Sullivan-Burstein, K. (1997). Homework how-to's. *Teaching Exceptional Children, 29,* 32–37.

Buell, B. G., & Buell, N. A. (1987). Perceptual modality preference as a variable in the effectiveness of continuing education for professionals (Doctoral dissertation, University of Southern California). *Dissertation Abstracts International, 48,* 283A.

Bursuck, W. D. (Ed.). (1995). *Homework: Issues and practices for students with learning disabilities.* Austin, TX: Pro.Ed.

Burwell, L. B. (1991). The interaction of learning styles with learner control treatments in an interactive videodisc lesson. *Educational Technology, 31*(3), 37–43.

Cai, J., Moyer, J. C., & Wang, N. (1997, March). *Parental roles in students' learning of mathematics.* Paper presented at the annual meeting of the American Educational Research Association, Chicago, IL.

Callan, R. J. (1996). Learning styles in the high school: A novel approach. *NASSP Bulletin, 80*(557), 66–71.

Campbell, B. J. (1991). Planning for a student learning style. *Journal of Education for Business, 66,* 356–359.

Campbell, L. J. (1990). *Using individual learning style inventories and group teaching methods in a sixth grade classroom.* Practicum report, Nova University, MI. (ERIC Document Reproduction Service No. ED 336 687)

Campbell, L. P. (1997). The consequences of freedom without structure. *Education, 118*(1), 56–58.

Canfield, A. A., & Lafferty, J. C. (1976). *Learning style inventory.* Detroit, MI: Humanics Media.

Cassidy, J., & Hossler, A. (1992, January/February). State and federal definitions of gifted: An update. *Gifted Child Today,* 46–53.

Caudill, G. (1998). Matching teaching and learning styles. *Technology Connection, 4*(8), 11, 24–25.

Chance, P. (1992). The rewards of learning. *Phi Delta Kappan, 74,* 200–207.

Chance, P. (1993). Sticking up for rewards. *Phi Delta Kappan, 74,* 787–790.

Chen, C., & Stevenson, H. W. (1989). Homework: A cross-cultural examination. *Child Development, 60,* 551–561.

Clariana, R. B. (1997). Considering learning style in computer-assisted learning. *British Journal of Educational Technology, 28*(1), 66–68.

Clark-Thayer, S. (1987). The relationship of the knowledge of student-perceived learning style preferences, and study habits and attitudes to achievement of college freshmen in a small urban university (Doctoral dissertation, Boston University, 1987). *Dissertation Abstracts International, 48,* 827A.

Cody, C. (1983). Learning styles, including hemispheric dominance: A comparative study of average, gifted and highly gifted students in grades five through twelve (Doctoral dissertation, Temple University). *Dissertation Abstracts International, 44,* 1631–6A.

Cohen, L. M., & Ambrose, D. C. (1993). Theories and practices for differentiated education for the gifted and talented. In K. A. Heller, F. J. Monks, & A. H. Passow (Eds.), *International handbook of research and development of giftedness and talent* (pp. 339–364). Oxford, Great Britain: Pergamon.

Cohen, V. L. (1997). Learning styles in a technology-rich environment. *Journal of Research on Computing in Education, 29,* 338–350.

Cool, V. A., & Keith, T. Z. (1991). Testing a model of school learning: Direct and indirect effects on academic achievement. *Contemporary Educational Psychology, 16*, 28–44.

Cooper, H. (1989a). *Homework*. White Plains, NY: Longman.

Cooper, H. (1989b). Synthesis of research on homework. *Educational Leadership, 47*(3), 85–91.

Cooper, H. (1994). *The battle over homework: An administrator's guide to setting sound and effective policies*. Thousand Oaks, CA: Corwin.

Cooper, H., Lindsay, J. J., Nye, B., & Greathouse, S. (1998). Relationships among attitudes about homework, amount of homework assigned and completed, and student achievement. *Journal of Educational Psychology, 90*, 70–83.

Cooper, H., & Nye, B. (1994). Homework for students with learning disabilities: The implications of research for policy and practice. *Journal of Learning Disabilities, 27*, 465–536.

Copenhaver, R. W. (1979). *The consistency of student learning styles as students move from English to mathematics*. Unpublished doctoral dissertation, Indiana University, Bloomington.

Cornett, C. W. (1983). *What should you know about teaching and learning styles*. Bloomington, IN: Phi Delta Kappa Foundation.

Corno, L. (1996). Homework is a complicated thing. Section 4: Grading the policymakers' solution. *Educational Researcher, 25*(8), 27–30.

Cross, J. A., Jr., (1982). Internal locus of control governs talented students (9–12). *Learning Styles Network Newsletter, 3*(3), 3.

Curry, L. (1987). *Integrating concepts of cognitive learning style: A review with attention to psychometric standards*. Ottawa, Ontario, Canada: Canadian College of Health Science Executives.

Curry, L. (1990). A critique of the research on learning styles. *Educational Leadership, 48*(2), 50–52, 54–56.

Davidman, L. (1981). Learning style: The myth, the panacea, the wisdom. *Phi Delta Kappan, 62*(9), 641–645.

DeBello, T. (1985). A critical analysis of the achievement and attitude effects of administrative assignments to social studies writing instruction based on identified, eighth-grade students' learning style preferences for learning alone, with peers, or with teachers (Doctoral dissertation, St. John's University). *Dissertation Abstracts International, 47*, 68A.

DeBello, T. C. (1990). Comparison of eleven major learning styles models: Variables, appropriate populations, validity of instrumentation, and the research behind them. *Reading, Writing, and Learning Disabilities, 6*, 203–222.

DeBello, T. C., & Guez, R. J. (1996). How parents perceive children's learning styles. *Principal, 76*(2), 38–39.

DeGregoris, C. N. (1986). Reading comprehension and the work recognition scores of seventh-grade students to provide supervisory and administrative guidelines for the organization of effective instructional environments (Doctoral dissertation, St. John's University). *Dissertation Abstracts International, 47*, 3380A.

Della-Valle, J., Dunn, K., Dunn, R., Geisert, G., Sinatra, R., & Zenhausern, R. (1986). The effects of matching and mismatching student's mobility preferences on recognition and memory tasks. *Journal of Educational Research, 79*, 267–272.

Dellas, M., & Gaier, E. L. (1970). Identification of Creativity: The individual. *Psychological Bulletin, 73*, 55–73.

Doyle, M. E., & Barber, B. S. (1990). *Homework as a learning experience* (3rd ed.). Washington, DC: National Education Association.

Dunlap, L. K., Dunlap, G., Koegel, L. K., & Koegel, R. L. (1991). Using self-monitoring to increase independence. *Teaching Exceptional Children, 23* (3), 17–22.

Dunn, R. (1989). Individualizing instruction for mainstreamed gifted children. In R. M. Milgram (Ed.), *Teaching gifted and talented learners in regular classrooms* (pp. 63–111). Springfield, IL: Charles C. Thomas.

Dunn, R. (1990). Understanding the Dunn and Dunn Learning Style Model and the need for individual diagnosis and prescription. *Reading, Writing, and Learning Disabilities, 6*, 223–247.

Dunn, R. (1992). Strategies for teaching word recognition to disabled readers. *Reading and Writing Quarterly, 8*, 157–177.

Dunn, R., Beaudry, J. S., & Klavas, A. (1989). Survey of research on learning styles. *Educational Leadership, 46*(6), 50–58.

Dunn, R., Deckinger, E. L., Withers, P., & Katzenstein, H. (1990). Should college students be taught how to do homework? The effects of studying marketing through individual perceptual strengths. *Illinois School Research and Development, 26*, 96–113.

Dunn, R., & Dunn, K. (1972). *Practical approaches to individualizing instruction: Contracts and other effective teaching strategies.* Nyack, NY: Parker.

Dunn, R., & Dunn, K. (1992). *Teaching elementary students through their individual learning styles: Practical approaches for grades 3–6.* Boston: Allyn & Bacon.

Dunn, R., & Dunn, K. (1993). *Teaching secondary students through their individual learning styles: Practical approaches for grades 7–12.* Boston: Allyn & Bacon.

Dunn, R., Dunn, K., & Price, G. E. (1979, 1981, 1984, 1987, 1989). *Learning style inventory.* Lawrence, KS: Price Systems.

Dunn, R., Ginnitti, M. C., Murray, J. B., Rossi, I., & Quinn, P. (1990). Grouping students for instruction: Effects of learning style on achievement and attitudes. *Journal of Social Psychology, 130*, 485–494.

Dunn, R., & Griggs, S. A. (1988). *Learning styles: Quiet revolution in American secondary schools.* Reston, VA: National Association of Secondary School Principals.

Dunn, R., and Griggs, S. A. (1990). Research on the learning style characteristics of selected racial and ethnic groups. *Reading, Writing, and Learning Disabilities, 6*, 261–280.

Dunn, R., Griggs, S. A., Olson, J., Beasley, M., & Gorman, B. S. (1995). A meta-analytic validation of the Dunn and Dunn model of learning style preferences. *Journal of Educational Research, 88*, 353–362.

Dunn, R., Griggs, S. A., & Price, G. E. (1993). Learning styles of Mexican American and Anglo-American elementary school students. *Journal of Multicultural Counseling and Development, 21*, 237–247.

Dunn, R., Krimsky, J., Murray, J., & Quinn, P. (1985). Light up their lives: A review of research on the effects of lighting on children's achievement. *The Reading Teacher, 38*(9), 863–869.

Dunn, R., & Milgram, R. M. (1993). Learning style of gifted students in diverse cultures. In R. M. Milgram, R. Dunn, & G. E. Price (Eds.), *Teaching gifted and talented perspective* (pp. 3–23). New York: Praeger.

Dunn, R., & Price, G. E. (1980). The learning style characteristics of gifted children. *Gifted Child Quarterly, 24,* 33–36.

Dunn, R., Price, G. E., Dunn, K., & Saunders, W. (1979). Relationship of learning style to self-concept. *The Clearing House, 53*(3), 155–158.

Epstein, J. (1990). Make language arts a family affair. *Instructor, 103*(5), 17.

Epstein, J. L. (1983). *Homework practices, achievement, and behaviors of elementary school students.* Baltimore: Johns Hopkins University. (ERIC Document Reproduction Service No. ED 250 351)

Epstein, J. L. (1985). Home and school connections in schools of the future: Implications of research on parent involvement. *Peabody Journal of Education, 62,* 18–41.

Epstein, J. L. (1998, April). *Interactive homework: Effective strategies to connect home and school.* Paper presented at the meeting of the American Educational Research Association, San Diego, CA.

Epstein, J. L., & Sanders, M. G. (1998). What we learn from international studies of school, family, and community partnerships. *Childhood Education, 74,* 392–394.

Epstein, M. H., Polloway, E. A., Buck, G. H., Bursuck, W. D., Wissinger, L. M., Whitehouse, F., & Jayanthi, M. (1997). Homework-related communication problems: Perspectives of general education teachers. *Learning Disabilities Research & Practice, 12,* 221–227.

Epstein, M. H., Polloway, E. A., Foley, R. M., & Patton, J. R. (1993). Homework: A comparison of teachers' and parents' perceptions of the problems experienced by students identified as having behavioral disorders, learning disabilities, or no disabilities. *Remedial and Special Education, 14,* 40–50.

Ferrari, J. R, Johnson, J. L., & McCown, W. G. (1995). *Procrastination and task avoidance theory, research, and treatment.* New York: Plenum.

Ferrari, J. R., Wesley, J. C., Wolfe, R. N., Erwin, C. N., Bamonto, S. M., & Beck, B. L. (1996). Psychometric properties of the revised Grasha-Riechmann Student Learning Style Scales. *Educational and Psychological Measurement, 56*(1), 166–172.

Finn, J. D. (1998). Parental engagement that makes a difference. *Educational Leadership, 55*(8), 20–24.

Fishman, B., Kupperman, J., & Soloway, E. (1998). Introducing urban Latino families to the internet at home: Preliminary issues and trends. In A. Bruckman, M. Guzdial, J. Kolodner, & A. Ram. (Eds.), *International conference on the learning sciences* (pp. 105–111). Atlanta, GA: AACE.

Fleming, N. D., & Mills, C. (1992). Not another inventory, rather a catalyst for reflections. *To Improve the Academy, 11,* 137–155.

Friedman, P., & Alley, R. (1984). Learning/teaching styles: Applying the principles. *Theory into Practice, 23*(1), 77–81.

Frith, G., (1991). Facilitating homework through effective support system. *Teaching Exceptional Children, 14*(5), 40–50.

Fucaloro, L., & Russikoff, K. (1998). *Assessing a virtual course: Development of a model.* (ERIC Document Reproduction Service No. ED 418 596)

Gagné, F. (1995). From giftedness to talent: A developmental model and its impact on the language of the field. *Roeper Review: A Journal on Gifted Education, 18,* 103–111.

Gajria, M., & Salend, S. J. (1995). Homework practices of students with and without learning disabilities: A comparison. In W. D. Bursuck (Ed.), *Homework: Issues and practices for students with learning disabilities* (pp. 97–106). Austin, TX: Pro.Ed.

Gardner, H. (1983). *Frames of mind: The theory of multiple intelligences.* New York: Basic Books.

Gill, B., & Schlossman, S. (1996). "A sin against childhood": Progressive education and the crusade to abolish homework, 1897–1941. *American Journal of Education, 105,* 27–66.

Grasha, A. G., & Riechmann, S. W. (1975). *Student Learning Styles Questionnaire.* Cincinatti, OH: University of Cincinatti Faculty Resource Center.

Gregorc, A. (1985). *Insider styles: Beyond the basics.* Columbia, CT: Gregorc Associates.

Gregorc, A. F. (1982). *Gregorc style delineator.* Maynard, MA: Gabriel Systems.

Griggs, S. A., & Price, G. E. (1980). A comparison between the learning styles of gifted versus average suburban junior high school students. *Roeper Review, 3,* 7–9.

Griss, S. (1998). *Minds in motion: A kinesthetic approach to teaching elementary curriculum. teacher-to-teacher series.* Portsmouth, NH: Heinemann.

Guskey, T. R. (1990). Integrating innovations. *Educational Leadership, 47* (5), 11–15.

Hayes, J., & Allison, C. W. (1993). Matching learning style and instructional strategy: An application of the person-environment interaction paradigm. *Perceptual and Motor Skills, 76,* 63–79.

Hecker, L. (1997). Walking, Tinkertoys, and Legos: Using movement and manipulatives to help students write. *English Journal, 86*(6), 46–52.

Heller, H. W., Spooner, F., Anderson, D., & Mims, A. (1988). Homework: A review of special education practices in the southwest. *Teacher Education and Special Education, 11,* 43–51.

Hill, J. E. (1976). *The educational sciences.* Bloomfield Hills, MI: Oakland Community College Press.

Hodgin, J., & Wooliscroft, C. (1997). Eric learns to read: Learning styles at work. *Educational Leadership, 54,* 43–45.

Hollifield, J. H. (1995). Parent involvement in middle schools. *Principal, 74*(3), 14–16.

Holmes, M., & Croll, P. (1989). Time spent on homework and academic achievement. *Educational Research, 31,* 36–45.

Hong, E. (1998, April). *Homework style, homework environment, and academic achievement.* Paper presented at the annual meeting of American Educational Research Association, San Diego, CA.

Hong, E., & Lee, K. (1999a, April). *Chinese parents' awareness of their children's homework style and homework behavior and its effect on achievement.* Paper presented at the annual meeting of the American Educational Research Association. Montreal, Canada.

Hong, E., & Lee, K. (1999b, April). *Preferred homework style and homework environment in high- versus low-achieving Chinese students.* Paper presented at the annual meeting of the American Educational Research Association, Montreal, Canada.

Hong, E. *A comprehensive model of giftedness*. Manuscript in preparation.

Hong, E., & Milgram, R. M. (1996). The structure of giftedness: The domain of literature as an exemplar: *Gifted Child Quarterly, 40*, 31–40.

Hong, E., & Milgram, R. M. (1998). *Homework Motivation and Preference: Questionnaire*. Las Vegas: University of Nevada, College of Education, and Tel Aviv, Israel: Tel Aviv University, School of Education.

Hong, E., & Milgram, R. M. (1999). Preferred and actual homework style: A cross-cultural examination. *Educational Research, 41*, 251–265.

Hong, E., Milgram, R. M., & Gorsky, H. (1995). Original thinking as a predictor of creative performance in young children. *Roeper Review, 18*, 147–149.

Hong, E., Milgram, R. M., & Perkins, P. G. (1995). Homework style and homework behavior of Korean and American Children. *Journal of Research and Development in Education, 28*, 197–207.

Hong, E., Milgram, R. M., & Whiston, S. C. (1993). Leisure activities in adolescents as a predictor of occupational choice in young adults: A longitudinal study. *Journal of Career Development, 19*, 221–229.

Hong, E., & Suh, B. K. (1995). An analysis of change in Korean-American and Korean students' learning styles. *Psychological Reports, 76*, 691–699.

Hong, E., Tomoff, J., Wozniak, E., Carter, S., & Topham, A. (2000). *Parent and student attitudes toward homework intervention and their effects on homework achievement and attitude*. Paper presented at the American Educational Research Association, New Orleans, LA.

Hong, E., Topham, A., Carter, S., Wozniak, E., Tomoff, J., & Lee, K. (2000). *A cross-cultural examination of the kinds of homework children prefer*. Paper presented at the American Educational Research Association, New Orleans, LA.

Hong, E., Whiston, S. C., & Milgram, R. M. (1993). Leisure activities in career guidance for gifted and talented adolescents: A validation study of the Tel-Aviv Activities Inventory. *Gifted Child Quarterly, 37*, 65–68.

Hoover-Dempsey, K. V., Bassler, O. C., & Burow, R. (1995). Parents' reported involvement in students' homework: Strategies and practices. *Elementary School Journal, 95*, 435–450.

Horowitz, F. D., & O'Brien, M. (Eds.). (1985). *The gifted and talented: Developmental perspectives*. Washington, DC: American Psychological Association.

Hughes, J. A. (1992). Review of the Learning Style Inventory [Price systems, Inc.]. In J. J. Kramer & J. C. Conoley (Eds.), *The 11th Mental Measurements Yearbook* (pp. 460–461). Lincoln: The Buros Institute of Mental Measurements, University of Nebraska-Lincoln.

Hunt, D. E. (1975). Person–environment interaction: A challenge found wanting before it was tried. *Review of Educational Research, 45*, 209–230.

Ingham, J. (1989). *An experimental investigation of the relationships among learning style perceptual preference, instructional strategies, training achievement, and attitudes of corporate employees*. Unpublished doctoral dissertation, St. John's University, New York.

James, W. B., & Galbraith, M. W. (1984). Perceptual learning styles of older adults. *Journal of Applied Gerontology, 3*(2), 214–218.

Janos, P. M., & Robinson, N. M. (1985). Psychosocial development in intellectually gifted children. In F. D. Horowitz & M. O'Brien (Eds.), *The gifted and talented: Developmental perspectives* (pp. 149–195). Washington, DC: American Psychological Association.

Jayanthi, M., Bursuck, W., Epstein, M. H., & Polloway, E. (1997). Strategies for successful homework. *Teaching Exceptional Children, 30*(1), 4–7.

Jenson, W. R., Sheridan, W. M., Olympia, D., & Andrews, D. (1995). Homework and students with learning disabilities and behavior disorders: A practical, parent-based approach. In W. D. Bursuck (Ed.)., *Homework: Issues and practices for students with learning disabilities* (pp. 107–123). Austin, TX: Pro.Ed.

Jeter, J., & Chauvin, J. (1982). Individualized instruction: Implications for the gifted. *Roeper Review, 5,* 2–3.

Jonassen, D. H., & Grabowski, B. L. (1993). *Handbook of individual differences, learning, and instruction.* Hillsdale, NJ: Lawrence Erlbaum.

Jones, R. D., & Ross, C. (1964). Abolish homework: Let supervised schoolwork take its place. *Clearing House, 39,* 206–209.

Kagan, J., Moss, H. A., & Sigel, I. E. (1963). The psychological significance of styles of conceptualization. In J. F. Wright & J. Kagan (Eds.), Basic cognitive processes in children. *Monograph of the Society for Research in Child Development, 28,* 73–112.

Kalous, T. D. (1990). Helping college students change their learning styles. *Journal of College and Adult Reading and Learning, 1*(1), 54–63.

Kavale, K. A., Hirshoren, A., & Forness, S. R. (1998). Meta-analytic validation of the Dunn and Dunn model of learning-style references: A critique of what was Dunn. *Learning Disabilities Research and Practice, 13*(2), 75–80.

Kay, P. J., Fitzgerald, M., Paradee, C., & Millencamp, A. (1995). Making homework work at home: The parent's perspective. In W. D. Bursuck (Ed.), *Homework: Issues and practices for students with learning disabilities* (pp. 125–146). Austin, TX: Pro.Ed.

Keefe, J. W. (1982). Assessing student learning styles. In J. W. Keefe (Ed.), *Student learning styles and brain behavior* (pp. 1–18). Reston, VA: National Association of Secondary School Principals.

Keefe, J. W. (Ed.). (1988). *Profiling and utilizing learning style.* Reston, VA: National Association of Secondary School Principals.

Keefe, J. W., & Monk, J. S. (1986). *Learning style profile examiners' manual.* Reston, VA: National Association of Secondary School Principals.

Keith, T. Z. (1986). *Homework (Kappa Delta Phi Classroom Practice Series).* West Lafayette, IN: Kappa Delta Phi.

Keith, T. Z. (1998). *Homework in and out of school.* Paper presented at the meeting of the American Educational Research Association, San Diego, CA.

Keith, T. Z., & Benson, M. J. (1992). Effects of manipulable influences on high school grades across five ethnic groups. *Journal of Educational Research, 86,* 85–93.

Keith, T. Z., Reimers, T. M., Fehrmann, P. G., Pottebaum, S. M., & Aubey, L. W. (1986). Parental involvement, homework, and TV time: Direct and indirect effects on high school achievement. *Journal of Educational Psychology, 78,* 373–380.

Kerka, S. (1998). *Learning styles and electronic information: Trends and issues alerts.* (ERIC Document Reproduction Service No. ED 420 788)

Kogan, S., & Rueda, R. (1997, March). *Comparing the effects of teacher-directed home-work and student-centered homework on return rate and homework attitudes of minority learning disabled students.* Paper presented at the annual meeting of the American Educational Research Association, Chicago, IL.

Kohn, A. (1993). Rewards versus learning: A response to Paul Chance. *Phi Delta Kappan, 74,* 783–787.

Kolb, D. A. (1976). *Learning Style Inventory: Technical manual.* Boston, MA: McBer.

Kolb, D. A. (1984). *Experiential learning: Experience as the source of learning and development.* Englewood Cliffs, NJ: Prentice Hall.

Lenehan, M. C., Dunn, R., Inghan, J., Signer, B. & Murray, J. B. (1994). Effects of learning-style intervention on college students' achievement, anxiety, anger and curiosity. *Journal of College Student Development, 35,* 461–466.

Letteri, C. A. (1980). Cognitive profile: Basic determinant of academic achievement. *Journal of Educational Research, 73,* 195–199.

Leiden, L. I., & Crosby, R. D., & Follmer, H. (1990). Assessing learning-style inventories and how well they predict academic performance. *Academic Medicine, 65,* 395–401.

Leung, J. J. (1993). *Chinese-Canadian children's attitudes toward schoolwork and perception of parental behaviors that support schoolwork.* (ERIC Document Reproduction Service No. ED 357 857)

Lowenfeld, V. (1987). *Creative and mental growth* (8th ed.). New York: Macmillan.

Ma, X. (1996). The effects of cooperative homework on mathematics achievement of Chinese high school students. *Educational Studies in Mathematics, 31,* 379–387.

MacMurren, H. (1985). A comparative study of the effects of matching and mismatching sixth-grade students with their learning style preferences for the physical element of intake and their subsequent reading speed and accuracy scores and attitudes (Doctoral dissertation, St. John's University). *Dissertation Abstracts International, 46,* 3247A.

Maeroff, G. (1989). *The school-smart parent.* New York: Times Books.

Maeroff, G. (1992). Reform comes home: Policies to encourage parental involvement in children's education. In C. Finn, Jr. & T. Rebarber (Eds.), *Education reform in the '90s* (pp. 157–174). New York: Macmillan.

Marino, J. F. (1993). Homework: A fresh approach to a perennial problem. *Momentum, 24,* 69–71.

Martin, D., & Potter, L. (1998). How teachers can help students get their learning styles met at school and at home. *Education, 118,* 549–555.

Martini, M. (1986). An analysis of the relationships between and among computer-assisted instruction, learning style perceptual preferences, attitudes and the science achievement of seventh-grade students in a suburban, New York school district (Doctoral dissertation, St. John's University). *Dissertation Abstracts International, 47,* 87A.

McClung, L. W. (1998). *A study on the use of manipulatives and their effect on student achievement in a high school Algebra I class.* Master of Arts Thesis, Salem-Teikyo University, West Virginia. (ERIC Document Reproduction Service No. ED 425 077)

McInerney, V., McInerney, D. M., & Marsh, H. W. (1997). Effects of metacognitive strategy training within a cooperative group learning context on computer achievement and anxiety: An aptitude-treatment interaction study. *Journal of Educational Psychology, 89,* 686–695.

Mercer, C. D., & Mercer, A. R. (1993). *Teaching students with learning problems.* New York:Macmillan.

Messick, S. (1976). Personal styles and educational option. In S. Messick (Ed.), *Individuality in learning* (pp. 327–368). San Francisco: Jossey Bass.

Miles, B. (1987). An investigation of the relationships among the learning style sociological preferences of fifth- and sixth-grade students, selected inter-active classroom patterns and achievement in career awareness and career decision-making concepts (Doctoral dissertation, St. John's University). *Dissertation Abstracts International, 48,* 2527A.

Milgram, R. M. (1973, 1983, 1987, 1990, 1998). *Tel Aviv Activities and Accomplishments Inventory.* Ramat Aviv, Israel: Tel Aviv University, School of Education.

Milgram, R. M. (Ed.). (1989). *Teaching gifted and talented children learners in regular classrooms.* Springfield, IL: Charles C. Thomas.

Milgram, R. M. (Ed.). (1991). *Counseling gifted and talented children learners in regular classrooms.* Norwood, NJ: Ablex.

Milgram, R. M., Dunn, R., & Price, G. E. (Eds.). (1993). *Teaching gifted and talented learners for learning style: An international perspective.* New York: Praeger.

Milgram, R. M., & Hong, E. (1994). Creative thinking and creative performance in adolescents as predictors of creative attainments in adults: A follow-up study after 18 Years. In R. Subotnik & K. Arnold (Eds.), *Beyond Terman: Contemporary longitudinal studies of giftedness and talent* (pp. 212–228). Norwood, NJ: Ablex.

Milgram, R. M., Hong, E., Shavit, Y. W., & Peled, R. (1997). Out-of-school activities in gifted adolescents as a predictor of vocational choice and work accomplishment in young adults. *Journal of Secondary Gifted Education, 8,* 111–120.

Milgram, R. M., & Milgram, N. A. (1976). Creative thinking and creative performance in Israeli children. *Journal of Educational Psychology, 68,* 255–259.

Milgram, R. M. & Price, G. E. (1993). The learning styles of gifted adolescents in Israel. In R. M. Milgram, R. Dunn, & G. E. Price (Ed.), *Teaching gifted and talented learners for learning style: An international perspective* (pp. 137–148). New York: Praeger.

Miller, L. M., (1985). *Mobility as an element of learning style: The effect its inclusion or exclusion has on student performance in the standardized testing environment.* Unpublished master's dissertation, University of North Florida, Jacksonville.

Miller, D. L., & Kelley, M. L. (1994). The use of goal setting and contingency contracting for improving children's homework performance. *Journal of Applied Behavior Analysis, 27,* 73–84.

Mills, M., & Stevens, P. (1998). *Improving writing and problem solving skills of middle school students.* Master's Action Research Project, Saint Xavier University and IRI/Skylight, IL. (ERIC Document Reproduction Service No. ED 429 876)

Mims, A., Harper, C., Armstrong, S. W., & Savage, S. (1991). Effective instruction in homework for students with disabilities. *Teaching Exceptional Children, 24* (1), 42–44.

Murrain, P. (1983). Administrative determinations concerning facilities utilization and instructional grouping: An analysis of the relationships between selected thermal environments and preferences for temperature, an element of learning style, as they affect word recognition scores of secondary students (Doctoral dissertation, St. John's University). *Dissertation Abstracts International, 44,* 1749A.

Nelson, J. S., Epstein, M. H., Bursuck, W. D., Jayanthi, M., & Sawyer, V. (1998). The preferences of middle school students for homework adaptations made by general education teachers. *Learning Disabilities Research and Practice, 13,* 109–117.

Nicholls, J. G., McKenzie, M., & Shufro, J., (1995). Schoolwork, homework, life's work: The experience of students with and without learning disabilities. In W. O. Bursuck (Ed.), *Homework: Issues and practices for students with learning disabilities* (pp. 83–96). Austin, TX: Pro. Ed.

Oakes, J. (1989). What educational indicators? The care for assessing the school concept. *Educational Evaluation and Policy Analysis, 11* (2), 181–199.

Ohayon, Y. (1999). *Preferred and actual homework motivation and preference in high and low creative thinking children.* Unpublished master's thesis, Tel Aviv University, Tel Aviv, Israel.

Olshansky, B. (1995). Picture this: An arts-based literacy program. *Educational Leadership, 53* (1), 44–47.

Olympia, D., Sheridan, S. M., & Jenson, W. R. (1994). Homework: A natural means of home-school collaboration. *School Psychology Quarterly, 9,* 60–64.

Onwuegbuzie, A. J., & Daley, C. E. (1997). Learning style and achievement in a course on research methods. *Psychological Reports, 80,* 496–498.

Pajares, F. (1996). Self-efficacy beliefs in academic settings. *Review of Educational Research, 66,* 543–578.

Palardy, J. M. (1995). Another look at homework. *Principal, 74* (5), 32–33.

Paschal, R. A., Weinstein, J., & Walberg, H. J. (1984). The effects of homework on learning: A quantitative synthesis. *Journal of Educational Research, 78,* 97–104.

Patton, J. R. (1995). Practical recommendations for using homework with students. In W. D. Bursuck (Ed.), *Homework: Issues and practices for students with learning disabilities* (pp. 181–196). Austin, TX: Pro.Ed.

Patzelt, K. E. (1991). *Increasing homework completion through positive reinforcement.* Philadelphia: La Salle College.

Paulu, N., & Darby, L. B. (Eds.). (1998). *Helping your students with homework: A guide for teachers.* (ERIC Document Reproduction Service No. ED 416 037)

Pendergrass, R. A. (1985). Homework: Is it really a basic? *Clearing House, 58,* 310–314.

Perkins, P. G., & Milgram, R. M. (1996). Parent involvement in homework: A double-edged sword. *International Journal of Adolescence and Youth, 6,* 195–203.

Perrin, J. (1984). An experimental investigation of the relationships among the learning style sociological preferences of gifted and nongifted primary children, selected instructional strategies, attitudes, and achievement in problem solving and rote memorization (Doctoral dissertation, St. John's University). *Dissertation Abstracts International, 44*, 342A.

Perrin, J. (1985). Preferred learning styles make a difference. *The School Administrator*, 4216.

Pettigrew, F., & Buell, C. (1989). Preservice and experienced teachers' ability to diagnose learning styles. *Journal of Educational Research, 82*, 187–189.

Pierce, M. (1997). *Improving elementary students' motivation*. Master's Action Research Project, Saint Xavier University and IRI/Skylight Field-Based Master's Program, IL. (ERIC Document Reproduction Service No. ED 412 002)

Pintrich, P. R., & Schunk, D. H. (1996). *Motivation in education: Theory, research, and applications*. Englewood Cliffs, NJ: Prentice Hall.

Pizzo, J., Dunn, R., & Dunn, K. (1990). A sound approach to improving reading: Responding to students' learning styles. *Journal of Reading, Writing, and Learning Disabilities International, 6* (3), 249–260.

Polloway, E. A., Epstein, M. H., Bursuck, W. D., Jayanthi, M., & Cumblad, D. (1995). Homework practices of general education teachers. In W. D. Bursuck (Ed.), *Homework: Issues and practices for students with learning disabilities* (pp. 39–57). Austin, TX: Pro.Ed.

Polloway, E. A., Epstein, M. H., & Foley, R. (1992). A comparison of the homework problems of students with learning disabilities and non-handicapped students. *Learning Disabilities: Research and Practice, 7*, 203–209.

Pribble, C. J. (1993). A homework survey of regular education and special education teachers. Unpublished doctoral dissertation, University of Utah, Salt Lake City.

Price, B. (1995). Meaning through motion: Kinesthetic English. *English Journal, 84* (8), 46–51.

Price, G. E., Dunn, K., Dunn, R., & Griggs, S. A. (1981). Studies in students' learning styles. *Roeper Review, 4*, 223–226.

Price, G. E., Dunn, R., & Sanders, W. (1980). Reading achievement and learning style characteristics. *The Clearing House, 5*, 223–226.

Price, G. E., & Milgram, R. M. (1993). The learning styles of gifted adolescents around the world: Differences and similarities. In R. M. Milgram, R. Dunn, & G. E. Price (Eds.), *Teaching gifted and talented learners for learning style: An international perspective* (pp. 229–247). New York: Praeger.

Radencich, M. C., & Schumm, J. S. (1997). *How to help your child with homework: Every caring parent's guide to encouraging good study habits and ending the homework wars*. Minneapolis, MN: Free Spirit Publishing.

Reese, W. (1995). *The origins of the American high school*. New Haven, CT: Yale University Press.

Reetz, L. J. (1990/1991). Parental perceptions of homework. *Rural Educator, 12* (2), 14–19.

Reid, J. M. (1987). The learning style preferences of ESL students. *TESOL Quarterly, 21*, 87–111.

Renzulli, J. S. (1986). The three-ring conception of giftedness: A developmental model for creative productivity. In R. J. Sternberg & J. E. Davidson (Eds.), *Conceptions of giftedness* (pp. 53–92). New York: Cambridge University.

Renzulli, J. S., & Reis, S. M. (1998). Talent development through curriculum differentiation. *NASSP Bulletin, 82*(595), 61–64.

Restak, R. (1979). One picture is worth a thousand words? Not necessarily! *The Modern Language Journal, 60* (4), 160–168.

Retish, P., Hitchings, W., Horvath, M., & Schmalle, B. (1991). *Students with disabilities in the secondary school.* New York: Longman.

Ricca, J. (1983). *Curricular implications of learning style differences between gifted and non-gifted students.* Unpublished doctoral dissertation, State University of New York, Buffalo.

Riding, R. J., & Burt, J. M. (1982). Reading versus listening in children: The effects of extraversion and coding complexity. *Educational Psychology, 2,* 47–58.

Rillero, P., & Helgeson, S. L. (1995). *An evaluation of the use of hands-on science homework assignments by sixth grade students and their parents.* (ERIC Document Reproduction Service No. ED 382 478)

Roderique, T. W., Polloway, E. A., Cumblad C., Epstein, M. H., & Bursuch, W. D. (1995). Homework: A survey of policies in the United States. In W. D. Bursuck (Ed.)., *Homework: Issues and practices for students with learning disabilities* (pp. 27–37). Austin, TX: Pro.Ed.

Rosemond, J. K. (1990). *Ending the homework hassle: Understanding, preventing, and solving school performance problems.* New York: Andrews & McMeel.

Rosenberg, M. S., (1995). The effects of daily homework assignments on the acquisition of basic skills by students with learning disabilities. In W. D. Bursuck (Ed.), *Homework: Issues and practices for students with learning disabilities* (pp. 147–167). Austin, TX: Pro.Ed.

Runco, M. A., & Albert, R. S. (Eds.). (1990). *Theories of creativity.* Newbury Park, CA: Sage.

Salend, S. J., & Schliff, J. (1989a). An examination of the homework practices of teachers of students with learning disabilities. *Journal of Learning Disabilities, 22,* 621–623.

Salend, S. J., & Schliff, J. (1989b). The many dimensions of homework. *Academic Therapy, 23,* 397–403.

Schmeck, R. R., Ribich, F. D., & Ramanaih, N. (1977). Development of a self-report inventory for assessing individual differences in learning processes. *Applied Psychological Measurement, 1,* 413–431.

Schunk, D. H. (1991). Self-efficacy and academic motivation. *Educational psychologist, 26,* 207–231.

Shields, J. M., & Heron, T. E. (1989). Teaching organizational skills to students with learning disabilities. *Teaching Exceptional Children, 21,* 8–13.

Silverman, L. K. (1989). Invisible goals, invisible handicaps. *Roeper Review, 12,* 37–41.

Sims, R. R., & Sims, S. J. (Eds.). (1995). *The importance of learning styles: Understanding the implications for learning, course design, and education.* Westport, CT: Greenwood Press.

Sims, R. R., Veres, J. G., & Locklear, T. (1991). An investigation of a modified version of Kolb's Revised Learning Style Inventory. *Educational and Psychological Measurement, 5*(1), 143–150.

Sims, S. J., & Sims, R. R. (1995). Learning and learning styles: A review and look to the future. In R. R. Sims & S. J. Sims (Eds.), *The importance of learning styles: Understanding the implications for learning, course design, and education* (pp. 193–210). Westport, CT: Greenwood Press.

Smith, T. E. (1990). Time and academic achievement. *Journal of Youth and Adolescence, 19*, 539–558.

Smock, S. M., & McCormick, S. M. (1995). Assessing parents' involvement in their children's schooling. *Journal of Urban Affairs, 17*, 395–411.

Snow, C. E., Barnes, W. S., Chandler, J., Goodman, I. F., & Hemphill, L. (1991). *Unfulfilled expectations: Home and school influences on literacy.* Cambridge, MA: Harvard University Press.

Sparks, B. I. (1990). The Kolb Learning Styles Inventory: Predicting academic potential among optometry students. *Journal of Optometric Education, 15*(2), 52–55.

Sternberg, R. J., & Davidson, J. E. (1986). *Conceptions of giftedness.* New York: Cambridge University Press.

Stewart, E. D. (1981). Learning styles among gifted/talented students: Instructional technique preferences. *Exceptional Children, 48*, 113–138.

Stipek, D. J. (1993). *Motivation to learn: From theory to practice* (2nd ed.). Boston, MA: Allyn & Bacon.

Stormont-Spurgin, M. (1997). I lost my homework: Strategies for improving organization in students with ADHD. *Intervention in School and Clinic, 32*, 270–274.

Strukoff, P. M., McLaughlin, T. F., & Bialozor, R. C. (1987). The effects of a daily report card system in increasing homework completion and accuracy in a special education setting. *Techniques: A Journal for Remedial Education and Counseling, 3*, 19–26.

Studd, M. (1995). Learning style differences: A student's point of view. *Clearing House, 69*(1), 38–39.

Sullivan, K., & Bryan, T. (1995). *Sequenced study skills program.* Phoenix, AZ: Planning for Success.

Swanson, D. P. (1992). ICAN: An acronym for success. *Teaching Exceptional Children, 28*(2), 22–26.

Swap, S. M. (1993). *Developing home-school partnerships: From concepts to practice.* New York: Teachers College Press.

Tannenbaum, A. J. (1983). *Gifted children: Psychological and educational perspectives.* New York: Macmillan.

Terman, L. M. (1925). *Genetic studies of genius: Mental and physical traits of a thousand gifted children.* Stanford, CA: Stanford University Press.

Terman, L. M., & Oden, M. H. (1947). *Genetic studies of genius: Vol. 4. The gifted child grows up: Twenty-five years follow-up of a superior group.* Stanford, CA: Stanford University Press.

Terman, L. M., & Oden, M. H. (1959). *Genetic studies of genius: Vol. 4. The gifted child at mid-life: Thirty-five years follow-up of the superior child.* Stanford, CA: Stanford University Press.

Trammel, D. L., Schloss, P. J., & Alper, S. (1995). Using self-recording, evaluation, and graphing to increase completion of homework assignments. In W. D. Bursuck (Ed.)., *Homework: Issues and practices for students with learning disabilities* (pp. 169–180). Austin, TX: Pro.Ed.

U.S. Department of Education. (1992). *Fourteenth Annual Report to Congress on the*

Implementation of the Individuals with Disabilities Education Act. Washington, DC: Author.

Walberg, H. J. (1984). Improving the productivity of America's schools. *Educational Leadership, 41*(8), 19–27.

Walberg, H. J., Paschal, R. A., & Weinstein, T. (1985). Homework's powerful effects on learning. *Educational Leadership, 42*, 76–78.

Wallace, J. (1995). Learning styles in the Philippines. *Education, 115*(4), 552.

Wallach, M. A., & Wing, C. W., Jr. (1969). *The talented student: A validation of the creativity-intelligence distinction*. New York: Holt, Rinehart, & Winston.

Warton, P. M. (1997). Learning about responsibility: Lessons from homework. *British Journal of Educational Psychology, 67*, 213–221.

Wasson, F. (1980). *A comparative analysis of learning styles and personality characteristics of achieving and underachieving gifted elementary students*. Unpublished doctoral dissertation, Florida State University, Tallahassee.

Westman, A. S. (1992). Review of the Learning Style Inventory [Price systems, Inc.]. In J. J. Kramer & J. C. Conoley (Eds.), *The 11th Mental Measurements Yearbook* (pp. 461–462). Lincoln. The Buros Institute of Mental Measurements, University of Nebraska-Lincoln.

Wing, C. W., Jr., & Wallach, M. A. (1971). *College admissions and the psychology of talent*. New York: Holt, Rinehart & Winston.

Witkin, H. A. (1976). Cognitive styles in academic performance and in teacher-student relations. In S. Messic (Ed.), *Individuality in learning* (pp. 38–72). San Francisco, CA: Jossey-Bass.

Witkin, H., & Goodenough, D. (1977). Field-dependence and interpersonal behavior. *Psychological Bulletin, 84*, 661–689.

Wood, J. A. (1987). *Helping students with homework*. Dubuque, IA: Kendall/Hunt.

Worrell, F. C., Gabelko, N. H., Roth, D. A., & Samuels, L. K. (1999). Parents' reports on homework amount and problems in academically talented elementary students. *Gifted Child Quarterly, 43*, 86–94.

Wuthrick, M. A. (1990). Blue jays win! Crows go down in defeat. *Phi Delta Kappan, 71*(7), 553–556.

Yong, F. L., & McIntyre, J. D. (1992). A comparative study of the learning style preferences of students with learning disabilities and students who are gifted. *Journal of Learning Disabilities, 25*, 124–132.

Zentall, S. S., Harper, G. W., & Stormont-Spurgin, M. (1993). Children with hyperactivity and their organizational deficits. *Journal of Educational Research, 97*, 112–117.

Index